PhotoPlus X6
Resource Guide

Contacting Serif

Contacting Serif Support

Our support mission is to provide fast, friendly technical advice and support from a team of experts.

Serif Support on the web

Service and Support   http://support.serif.com/

🐦 Twitter   twitter.com/serifsupport

📘 Facebook   http://www.facebook.com/SerifSupport

Additional Serif information

Serif website   http://www.serif.com

Forums   http://forums.serif.com

📺 YouTube   http://youtube.com/serifsoftware

Main office (UK, Europe)

The Software Centre, PO Box 2000, Nottingham, NG11 7GW, UK

Phone   (0115) 914 2000

Phone (Registration)   (0800) 376 1989

Phone (Sales)   (0800) 376 7070

Phone (Service and Support)   0845 345 6770

Fax   (0115) 914 2020

North American office (US, Canada)

Phone (Registration)   800-794-6876

Phone (Sales)   800-489-6703

Phone (Customer Service)   800-489-6720

Support   603-886-6642

For international enquiries, please contact our main office.

Credits

This Resource Guide, and the software described in it, is furnished under an end user License Agreement, which is included with the product. The agreement specifies the permitted and prohibited uses.

Trademarks

Serif is a registered trademark of Serif (Europe) Ltd.

PhotoPlus is a registered trademark of Serif (Europe) Ltd.

All Serif product names are trademarks of Serif (Europe) Ltd.

Microsoft, Windows and the Windows logo are registered trademarks of Microsoft Corporation. All other trademarks acknowledged.

Windows Vista and the Windows Vista Start button are trademarks or registered trademarks of Microsoft Corporation in the United States and/or other countries.

Adobe Photoshop is a registered trademark of Adobe Systems Incorporated in the United States and/or other countries.

Copyrights

Introduction

Welcome to the PhotoPlus X6 Resource Guide.

This Resource Guide covers the best techniques for using the fundamental tools in PhotoPlus from beginner- to advanced-level and provides creative inspiration for your photo projects.

1: Adjusting Photos

This chapter provides exercises to help you process your raw images and use key post-processing adjustments such as levels and curves. It includes information on resizing, cropping, straightening, sharpening, combining and tinting photos as well as applying digital makeup to portraits.

2: Creative Effects

These project-based tutorials show you how to work with a range of PhotoPlus X6 tools, including layers and masks, to create artistic effects. Projects include creating a Tilt-Shift miniature, a typographic portrait, a watercolour, and applying a 1970s retro effect.

3: Final Touches

Once your photos look perfect and your artistic compositions are complete, these tutorials provide you with suggestions on how to finish your projects off before sharing them with friends, family and clients. They walk you through adding stylized edges, copyrights and captions, and, most importantly, saving and exporting your photos.

4: Creative Showcase

Be inspired by the work in this chapter! The examples were created using brushes from the Brush Tips tab and the presets in PhotoFix and the Filter Gallery. A selection of samples provided with PhotoPlus are also shown. Instructions on accessing these areas of PhotoPlus are included.

Working with tutorials

You will need a variety of photos to be able to work through the tutorials in this Resource Guide. For some tutorials, we have provided one or more resource files to get you started.

Accessing the resource files

All resource files are free and are accessible via the Internet at the following location:

> http://go.serif.com/resources/HPX6

Once you've clicked on a file, you can either open or save it. We recommend you save the file to your desktop or a named folder on your computer.

Useful icons

Before we get started, here is a quick guide to the icons that you'll find useful along the way.

When you see this icon, there are project files and/or images available for download that will help you to complete the tutorial. Sometimes we provide you with partially completed projects so that you can concentrate on the main learning point of the tutorial, without having to recreate our design.

Don't forget to save your work! It's good practice to save often. We'll remind you along the way with these helpful save points.

These give you an estimate of how long a tutorial will take to complete. Some tutorials are longer than others so this should help you put enough time aside to complete a tutorial.

Not sure how hard a tutorial is? Let the pencils guide you. Tutorials are graded between 1 (beginner) - 5 (advanced). This provides a guide to how much PhotoPlus experience is recommended before attempting the tutorial. Don't worry though, nothing is impossible and you should always be able to follow the steps!

This is a note. Notes provide useful information about the program or a particular technique.

This is a tip. Our tips provide information that will help you with your projects.

This is a warning! We don't want to make you panic but when you see this icon, you need to pay attention to the steps as they will be particularly important.

Further Resources

There are a range of further resources available to help you get the most from PhotoPlus.

- Online video tutorials
  These videos guide you through a range of techniques for using the tools available in PhotoPlus.
  Available from the PhotoPlus Startup Wizard's **Learn** section.

- Comprehensive PhotoPlus Help
  The PhotoPlus Help provides information and instructions on using all the tools, features, and settings within PhotoPlus.
  Available via the **Help** menu (or press the **F1** key).

- How To tab
  The How To tab provides basic information about PhotoPlus tools and features, and includes step-by-step instructions and automated assistance.
  Available within PhotoPlus (displayed on the left-hand side by default).

Exploring PhotoPlus X6

(A) Standard toolbar, (B) How To tab, (C) Tools toolbar, (D) Image "canvas", (E) Hintline toolbar, (F) Documents tab, (G) Snapping toggle, (H) Layers, Channels, & Macros tabs, (I) Adjustments, Brush Tip, & History tabs, (J) Histogram, Navigator, & Colour tabs, (K) Context toolbar.

The PhotoPlus workspace

The PhotoPlus studio workspace consists of:

- Your image canvas.

- The **Documents** tab, which displays all of your open images.

- The **How To** tab, where many commands can be applied automatically.

- A range of image-specific **tabs**, to help you organize your workflow and make image adjustments.

- Horizontal and vertical **toolbars**, used to access PhotoPlus commands and tools.

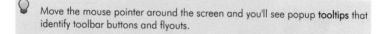

Move the mouse pointer around the screen and you'll see popup **tooltips** that identify toolbar buttons and flyouts.

Right-click any object or page region to bring up a **context menu** of functions.

Contents

Creative Showcase **197**

Adjusting Photos

Whether you're a novice, amateur or professional photographer, you'll always have photos which would benefit from some type of modification. Some photos will only need a minor tweak to get them looking fantastic while others require substantial work. We'll show you the steps necessary to get that picture looking perfect.

Raw Images

 20 min

When you take a photo as a raw file, you are essentially saving an unprocessed image. It's basically a digital negative and needs to be developed. PhotoPlus has a digital dark room called Import Raw for just this purpose.

In this tutorial, we'll look at some basic corrections and settings that you apply to your raw file in the Import Raw dialog.

 Unfortunately, as raw files are so large, we can't provide a file for you to use, but the steps in the tutorial will work with any image with similar exposure problems. Remember, there are no hard and fast rules. Corrections are mainly done by eye and need to be adjusted to each individual photo.

By the end of this tutorial you will be able to:

- Open a raw image file.

- Crop a photo.

- Adjust white balance and change exposure.

- Recover blown highlights.

- Improve sharpness and reduce noise.

Let's begin...

We'll start with a photo of a duck which was simultaneously taken as a JPEG and raw file.

The image above shows how heavily underexposed the JPEG was. Luckily, we can use the raw file to allow us to make adjustments to dramatically improve the exposure.

To open a raw image:

* Click **Open** on the Standard toolbar and then browse to your raw file.

    - or -

* Drag and drop a raw file from Windows Explorer onto the empty workspace.

The image opens in the **Import Raw** dialog.

All we need to do is fine-tune it by correcting the white-balance, the noise and a slight tweak to the exposure. But first, it's best to crop the photo to the size you want.

Cropping

The main reason for cropping a photo is to improve its overall composition. However, if you crop before doing any other corrective procedures, it will help you better evaluate the adjustments needed. Cropping unwanted areas will mean you can focus adjustments on the desirable area only, therefore getting the best from the settings you apply. Let's take a look at this now.

 Cropping in the **Import Raw** dialog is destructive, unlike using the **Crop Tool** in PhotoPlus's main workspace. For more details on cropping photos, see *Learning to Crop* on p. 25, or search *Importance of cropping* and *Cropping an image* in PhotoPlus Help.

To crop an image:

1. On the **Retouch Tools** toolbar, click the ◰ Crop and Straighten tool.

2. On the **Crop** section, select 🔒 lock to ensure the **Aspect Ratio** remains as **Original**.

3. In the preview window, drag the corner handles of the crop area to position the crop (using the thirds grid as a guide—search *Rule of Thirds* in PhotoPlus Help for more information)

4. When you're happy with the crop, click ✅ **Accept**.

Not only can you see the difference in the composition, you will also notice the difference in the photo's histogram.

White balance

Our image has a green cast. We can see this in the image itself and by looking at the left-hand histogram.

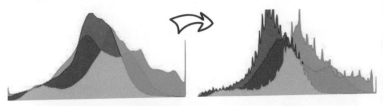

To correct the white balance:

1. From the **Filters: Global**, on the **White Balance** filter, click the ✎ **Set white level**.

2. Click on a light area of your image that should be a neutral reference point.

The colour balance is updated. If it's not quite right, click on another area until a natural colour balance is achieved.

Notice that the histogram is also updated to show the change in tonal balance (see above, right-hand histogram).

Changing exposure

If the image is still too dark, we can use the sliders to increase the exposure more. It's important to be careful not to do this too much otherwise you risk losing detail in the lighter areas of the image.

In our example, an **Exposure** adjustment of 0.1 is enough just to lift the image a little more.

To increase the image exposure:

1.   From the **Filters: Global**, on the **Lighting** filter, increase the **Exposure** by dragging the slider.

Aim for small increments and let the preview pane update each time before you make further adjustments.

2. Ideally, keep an eye on the histogram and make sure that you stop before clipping occurs at the right edge. Sometimes, as in our example, clipping is unavoidable if you want to bring out the detail in the darker areas.

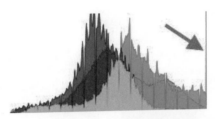

Notice that the histogram has spread out again while retaining the shape it had after the white balance adjustment.

Highlight recovery

In the previous example, we had underexposed the photo. But what if you photo is overexposed and as a result the highlights have been lost or "clipped"? Raw files store a little extra data about exposure. This means that if an image was slightly overexposed, you can recover a certain amount of the exposure data. Again, the Import Raw dialog can come to our rescue!

In the Import Raw dialog, the levels have been partially corrected. However, if we look closely at the right side of the histogram, we can see that there is a peak right at the edge. This tells us that the image has "blown" or "clipped" highlights.

Ideally, we don't want to reduce the exposure overall as the rest of the photo is well exposed. In this case, we need to use highlight recovery.

To recover highlights:

1. From the **Filters: Global**, on the **Highlights** filter, select **Recovery** from the **Mode** drop-down list.

2. Begin with a **Strength** setting of 1 and gradually increase it until the detail starts to appear in the blown section.

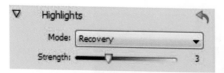

The entire photo will get slightly darker, but we can correct this later.

At a strength of 3, the detail has appeared in the feathers.

3. Notice that the histogram has been "squashed" and the clipping has been greatly reduced.

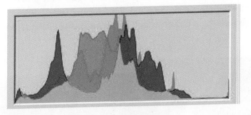

 As you increase the highlight recovery strength, you may notice a greater level of colour casting. However, this can easily be fixed by a **Colour Balance** adjustment in PhotoPlus. Search *Colour Balance adjustment* in PhotoPlus Help.

You may find that you'll need to readjust the white balance or sharpen the image. We'll return to our originally underexposed duck photo to show the Unsharp Mask adjustment.

Sharpening

The sharpness of our duck photo is pretty good but, at higher zoom levels, there is a little too much softness around the edges. An Unsharp Mask works mainly to enhance the edges in an image. We'll apply this adjustment now.

To sharpen:

1. From the **Filters: Global**, click ☐ **Enable** to activate the **Unsharp Mask** filter.

    The **Unsharp Mask** filter will be applied at the default settings.

2. To adjust the settings, clicking the ▷ **Expand/Collapse filter** arrow next to the filter and then increase or decrease the **Amount** setting to strengthen or weaken the sharpen effect, respectively—we set ours to 100%.

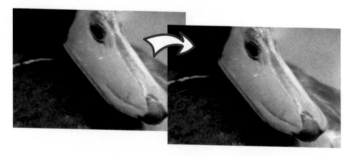

Our photo already suffered from noise and the Unsharp Mask accentuated this, as you can see in the above example. This can be fixed with the noise reduction adjustment.

Noise reduction

Photos taken using a high ISO setting, or those that are underexposed like our example, often suffer with "digital noise". Noise is normally displayed as pixels of an unexpected, often brighter colour.

We can reduce the noise in an image by using the noise reduction filter.

To reduce noise:

1. From the **Filters: Global**, click ☐ **Enable** to activate the **Noise Reduction** filter.

   The **Noise Reduction** filter will be applied at the default settings.

2. To adjust the settings, clicking the ▷ **Expand/Collapse filter** arrow next to the filter and then:

   - Increase the **Colour** slider to eradicate randomly placed colour pixels which constitute the most noticeable areas of noise.

   - Increase the **Luminance** slider to reduce areas where pixels are unnaturally lighter or darker than surrounding pixels.

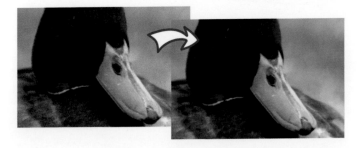

Importing into main workspace

With all your raw adjustments made, it's now time to complete the import of your file and open it in PhotoPlus's main workspace for saving, exporting or further adjusting.

To complete raw import:

- In the **Import Raw** dialog, set the **Output Format** using the **Bit Depth** and **Colour** drop-down lists, and then click **OK**.

   Your processed raw file opens in the workspace.

We left the format set to 16 Bits/Channel so we could continue to edit our photo at the highest quality resolution possible.

If you wish to apply further adjustments to your photo, check out *Key Adjustments* on p. 33. For more information on the settings available in the Import Raw dialog, search *Adjusting raw images* in PhotoPlus Help.

 Exporting your completed image to a common image file format will allow you to get full use from it. See *Saving & Exporting* on p. 187 for more information.

Resizing & Resampling

⏱ 5-15 min 🖊🖊🖊🖊🖊

There may be times when you want to use a photo but it's too big or too small for the purpose. The best way to solve this problem is to resize (or resample) the photo. We'll show you how in this tutorial.

By the end of this tutorial you will be able to:

• Resize (scale) a photo for print.

• Resample a photo for print.

• Resample an image for screen viewing.

• Optimize file sizes for websites and sharing.

Let's begin...

1.   On the Standard toolbar, click  **Open**.

2.   Locate your chosen photo and click **Open**.

The photo opens in the workspace.

Our photo was taken using a digital camera and measures 2509 x 1754 pixels.

Resizing vs Resampling

A typical monitor resolution is either 72 pixels per inch (ppi) or 96 ppi. This is what controls an image's size on screen. When you print a photo, the pixels are printed as small dots. The number of dots per inch gives a photo its dpi setting. A high quality photo print will be printed at 300 dots per inch (dpi).

There are two ways to change the size of an image—resizing and resampling. What's the difference? Although often used interchangeably, there's actually an important difference between the two.

- **Resizing**, otherwise known as scaling, changes the size at which the photo will print, without changing the number of pixels in the photo. Resizing determines whether the pixels are printed further apart (to print it bigger) or closer together (to print it smaller). Resizing an image will not affect screen display.

- **Resampling** changes the number of pixels in the photo. This is the only way that you can change the size at which an image will display on screen. When resampling, dpi settings are ignored.

  For printing small photos at an increased size, you may need to resample them first while maintaining a certain dpi print resolution.

Both methods are available in PhotoPlus via the Image Size dialog.

Resizing photos for print

The only time that you'll really resize (scale) a photo is when you want to
print it. Remember, resizing does not modify the photo in any way.
Obviously, to get a good print you'll need to maintain a certain dpi—
200dpi will produce an excellent home print; aim for 300dpi for a
professional print.

To resize (scale) a photo:

1. From the Image menu, click **Image Size**.

The Image Size dialog opens.

2. Clear the **Resize layers** option. All resampling options are greyed
out.

In the Print Size section, the current Width, Height and Resolution
dimensions are displayed.

The native resolution of our photo is 96 dpi. At this resolution, as the
dialog shows us, the photo will print at approximately 26 x 18
inches.

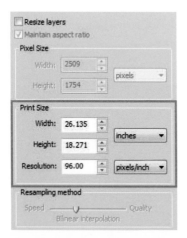

3.   To force the photo to print at 300dpi, in the **Resolution** box, type '300' and press the **Tab** key.

The printing Width and Height update automatically to approximately 8.4 x 5.8 inches.

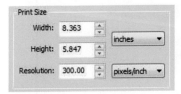

4.   Alternatively, to specify exact print dimensions, in the **Width** box, type the width you want the photo to print at (e.g. 12.5) and press the **Tab** key.

The Height and Resolution values will update to match.

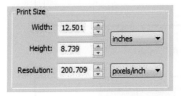

5.   When you are happy with the print size, click **OK**.

At first it might seem like nothing has changed. This is somewhat true! Your photo remains unaltered and your monitor still displays it at its native resolution. However, the change is apparent when you come to print it.

The following illustrations show how our photo will print with the two settings we mentioned above.

8.4 x 5.8 inches at 300 dpi on A3 paper

12.5 x 8.7 inches at 200 dpi on A3 paper

The photo's dimensions have been compressed or expanded to change the size of the printed photo, but the photo itself remains unchanged. Try printing a copy to see the effects.

 If you use the ✄ **Crop Tool** to specify printed dimensions (see *Learning to Crop* on p. 25), not only are the unwanted areas cropped away, but PhotoPlus also resizes (scales) the photo by changing the dpi to fit the specified print size. The following screenshot shows the dimensions of our photo after a 7x5 crop. The aspect ratio has changed (the width is shorter) but the rest of the photo is the same. However, the **Resolution** (dpi) is increased in order to obtain the 7 inch x 5 inch print.

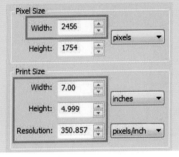

Resampling images for print, screen, email and the Web

There are many times when you want to create a larger or smaller version of your photo—to create a large, high quality print, to create a small file to share via email, or to create a lower resolution image for your website. In each case, you'll need to change the number of pixels in the actual photo, i.e. **resample** it. We'll show you how to do this without the distortion that resampling can sometimes introduce.

We'll start by creating a 300dpi A3 poster print of our photo. To ensure that the print goes right to the edges, we'll increase our image print size to approximately 12.5 inches x 18 inches.

To enlarge an image to a 300 dpi print by resampling:

1. From the Image menu, click Image Size.

2. In the Image Size dialog:

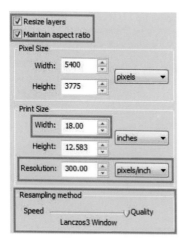

- Ensure the **Resize layers** option is selected.

- Ensure the **Maintain aspect ratio** option is selected.

- Drag the **Resampling method** slider to **Lanczos 3 Window** (this is the 'best' but slowest resampling method)

- In the **Print Size** section set the **Resolution** to 300.

- If necessary, set the required print **Width** or **Height**.

  If **Maintain aspect ratio** is selected (recommended), when you change the width, the height updates correspondingly and vice versa.

  As you can see, in our example the overall pixel size of the image is automatically increased from 2509 x 1754 to 5400 x 3775.

- Click **OK**.

3. PhotoPlus resamples the photo to the new size ready for printing.

After resampling a photo, you may need to sharpen the details. Try using the **Unsharp Mask** on the **Effects>Sharpen** menu to sharpen your photo before printing. For more on using the Unsharp Mask, see *Sharpening Blurred Photos* on p. 45.

Make sure you save your resampled image as a new file and be sure not to overwrite the original!

To change image dimensions for screen:

1. From the Image menu, click Image Size.

2. In the Image Size dialog:

    *   Ensure the **Resize layers** option is selected.

    *   Ensure the **Maintain aspect ratio** option is selected.

    *   Drag the **Resampling method** slider to **Lanczos 3 Window** (this is the 'best' but slowest resampling method)

    *   In the **Pixel Size** section set the required screen **Width** or **Height**—setting the largest dimension to around 800 pixels works well.

        If **Maintain aspect ratio** is selected (recommended), when you change the width, the height will automatically update and vice versa.

    *   Click **OK**.

 Remember, only pixel dimensions are important when resizing an image for screen viewing purposes as all dpi settings are ignored.

Resizing images when exporting

If you want to resize a photo for a specific reason, e.g. to add it to a website, you might find it easier to use the **Export Optimizer** dialog. On export, an entirely new copy of the photo is created, resampled to the dimensions you specify. This means you don't need to permanently resample your original photo.

We look at this process in full in *Saving & Exporting* on p. 187.

Learning to Crop

15 min

Every photo has boundaries, and you can decide where those boundaries should be. Cropping is an easy, yet often overlooked, step when editing photos. In this tutorial, we'll show you how to use the various tools in PhotoPlus to crop your photos to add visual impact and focus.

By the end of this tutorial you will be able to:

- Define a crop selection size using the Crop Tool.

- Use the Thirds Grid to aid photo composition.

- Crop to a pre-defined print size.

- Create a circular crop by cropping to a selection.

Let's begin...

1. On the Standard toolbar, click **Open**.

2. Locate a photo (ideally with a definite subject as this will be easier) and click **Open**.

    The image opens in the workspace.

Cropping an image

By default, when you crop a photo, PhotoPlus hides all of the pixels outside the crop selection area. The canvas size is automatically resized to show only the area inside the crop selection.

 Cropping can be switched to destructive mode, so pixels outside of the crop area are permanently discarded! The best approach is to save a copy of your photo first and apply the crop to the copy.

You can crop larger areas when photos are shot at a high resolution. Keep this in mind before taking photos and make sure your camera is set to its highest resolution and image quality.

To crop the image with Crop Tool:

1. On the Tools toolbar, select the ⬠ **Crop Tool**.

2. Drag out a rectangular crop selection area on the image. (To constrain the region to a square, hold down the **Ctrl** key while dragging.)

    The area that will be hidden turns dark.

3. If required, click and drag inside the selection to move the whole crop area (the cursor changes to the **Move** cursor), or drag the sizing handles to resize.

4. On the context toolbar, click to crop to the designated size (or double-click inside the selected area). The crop is applied.

Save now! Click **File > Save As** and choose a new name for your file.

> If you intend on making any further adjustments to your photo, it's worth saving the file as an .spp file. This will also allow you to increase the cropped area at a later date, if necessary.

Using the Rule of Thirds

The Crop Tool comes with a handy component which helps you compose your image by cropping while using the Rule of Thirds.

To use the Rule of Thirds grid:

1. On the Tools toolbar, select the ◫ **Crop Tool**.

2. On the context toolbar, select the **Thirds grid** option.

3.   Drag to define your crop area—a 3 x 3 grid is superimposed within your crop selection area.

For best results, position the subject of the photo at any of the four intersection points on the grid.

4.   Double-click inside the crop selection (or click  on the context toolbar) to crop to the outer grid dimensions.

As you can see, a close crop can completely enhance or change the focus of an image. For more information, search *Rule of Thirds* in PhotoPlus Help.

Save now! Click **File** > **Save As** and choose a new name for your file.

Cropping to a standard print size

Some digital photographs sizes do not comply with the standard print sizes—i.e. 6x4, 7x5, 8x10—but the Crop Tool comes with presets to help you crop specifically to these sizes and more.

To crop to a pre-defined print size:

1.   On the Tools toolbar, select the ⊠ Crop Tool.

2.   On the context toolbar, from the left-most drop-down list, choose a pre-defined print size. We chose **6 x 4 in**.

3.   Drag out to define your crop selection area.

4.   Double-click inside the crop selection to crop to the designated size.

The print resolution adjusts to honour the print dimensions. Now all you need to do is export your photo and send for professional printing (see *Saving & Exporting* on p. 187) or print at home directly from PhotoPlus (search *Printing* in PhotoPlus Help)!

 Save now! Click **File > Save As** and choose a new name for your file.

Creative Cropping

In PhotoPlus you can also crop to selections. This allows you to be more creative with your cropping. Let's look at this now...

 Cropping to a selection permanently discards the pixels outside of the crop area! The best approach is to save a copy of your photo first and apply the crop to the copy.

To crop to selection:

1.   On the Tools toolbar, from the Shape Selection Tools flyout, click the ⬭ **Ellipse Selection Tool.**

2. Hold down the **Ctrl** key and drag to define a circular crop selection area.

3. If required, click and drag inside the selection to reposition the selection area.

4. From the **Image** menu, click **Crop to Selection**.

 The area surrounding the crop will be filled with the background colour as set on the **Colour** tab. In the example above, the background colour was set to white.

Remember, the cropping to selection technique is not limited to a circular shape, it can be used to create any shaped crops! This technique can also be used to create rounded edged photos (see *Stylized Edges: Rounded edges* on p. 169 for an alternative technique).

Key Adjustments

 15 min

This tutorial takes you through the various methods you can use to straighten and enhance a photograph.

By the end of this tutorial you will be able to:

• Straighten an image.

• Apply a Vibrance adjustment to enhance colours.

• Make Levels and Curves adjustments.

Let's begin...

1.   On the Standard toolbar, click 📂 **Open**.

2.   Locate your chosen photo and click **Open**.

The photo opens in the workspace.

Now we can explore a few techniques to help enhance our photographs—beginning with some easy adjustments and then moving on to the professional favourites later in the tutorial.

Straightening/Cropping images

It's not always easy to get the horizon straight when taking photos, particularly when you're more focused on getting other elements right. However, sometimes even the slightest offset can confuse the eye and ruin a perfectly good photo. The Straighten Tool allows you to straighten the horizon instantly.

As you can see in our example, this idyllic coastal scene is ruined by the angle of the horizon—but we can get that rectified in seconds.

Straightening a photo is a permanent process—depending on the settings, some of the photo may be discarded! The best approach is to save a copy of your photo first and apply the straighten to the copy.

To straighten an image:

1. On the Tools toolbar, from the Crop Tools flyout, select the Straighten Tool.

2. On the context toolbar, from the Canvas drop-down list, ensure **Crop** is selected.

3. (Optional) If you're working on a multi-layer image and wish to straighten only the selected layer, ensure **Rotate All Layers** is not selected.

4. Click and drag a line across your image to define your new horizon.

Your photo will automatically realign according to the line you have defined and cropped to remove any empty areas resulting from the straighten adjustment.

A photo can sometimes be enhanced by cropping (covered in more details in *Learning to Crop* on p. 25).

Save now! Click **File > Save As** and choose a new name for your file.

Adjusting Vibrance

This adjustment subtly enriches the colours in your photo without saturating skin tones, giving an authentic, bold finish. Even the slightest increase can have a dramatic impact on your photo.

The yellow and orange tones in our photo could be improved by increasing their saturation. We could use a Hue/Saturation/Lightness adjustment, but we risk overtly affecting the bride's skin tone. To avoid this risk, we can use a Vibrance adjustment.

To apply a vibrance adjustment:

1. On the **Adjustments** tab, click **Vibrance**.

    A new adjustment layer is added.

2.   Increase the **Vibrance** slider to saturate photo colours while
     protecting skin tones.

As you can see in our worked example, the colours are now richer and
warmer, including the bride's blonde hair and red lips. Her skin tone has
been warmed lightly, but still retains its flesh tone. The Vibrance
adjustment can be more subtle, as with the Red Arrows example, the
coloured smoke is more dramatic and thicker.

Save now! Click **File > Save As** and choose a new name for your file.

Adjusting Levels

The Levels adjustment displays a histogram showing the proportion of
photo pixels at each lightness value, ranging from shadows through to
highlights. By looking at the histogram, you can see if the photo lacks a
'high end' or a 'low end,' and adjust the **black** or **white** point
accordingly.

Let's look at improving the levels of this nautical scene.

To apply a levels adjustment:

1. On the **Adjustments** tab, click **Levels**.

    A new adjustment layer is added.

2. The histogram on the **Adjustments** tab, in our example, shows that the image is lacking a low end. We can correct this by dragging the black point slider to the edge of the histogram (input level 32).

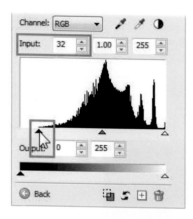

Immediately the image has a higher level of contrast with the water and ship appearing more defined.

Moreover, you can modify the Red, Green and Blue channels individually to give a richer, more refined finish.

To apply an advanced levels adjustment:

1.   On the **Adjustments** tab, click **Levels**.

2.   On the **Adjustments** tab, from the **Channel** drop-down list, select **Blue**.

     The histogram for the Blue channel only displays.

3.   In our example, while different to the RGB histogram, the Blue histogram is still lacking a low end. We can correct this by dragging the black point slider to the edge of the histogram.

4.   Repeat step 2, instead selecting the **Green** and **Red** channels, and then analyse the histograms and apply an appropriate adjustment.

By adjusting the level of each channel separately, the photo's blue haze has been completely eradicated!

 Save now! Click **File** > **Save As** and choose a new name for your file.

The Levels adjustment can also be used for creative effect, see *1970s Retro Effect* on p. 117 for an example of this.

Adjusting Curves

Probably the professional photographer's favourite adjustment. The Curves adjustment lets you correct the tonal range of a photo—the spread of lightness values through shadow, midtone, and highlight regions—and control individual colour components. It gives the greatest control of the midtones and when used carefully, really enhances a photo.

To apply a curves adjustment:

1. On the **Adjustments** tab, click **Curves**.

   A new adjustment layer is added.

2. The **Adjustments** tab shows the **Curves** graph:

   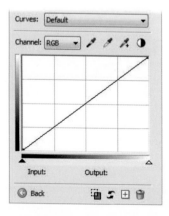

- (Optional) Click ✦ **Add Control Point** and then click on a light or dark area you want to adjust.

  A control point is added to the curves graph.

- Click and drag the curves line down to darken the midtones.

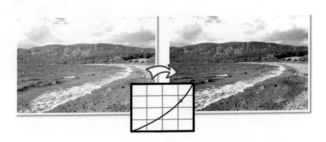

- Click and drag the curves line up to lighten the midtones.

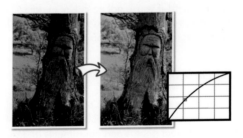

- For washed out images, you should aim for a gentle S-shape to deepen the shadows, lighten the highlights, and increase contrast.

You'll see these photos display a greater level of contrast, sharpened details, and boosted colours. Curves adjustments also work equally well with black and white (greyscale) images.

This is probably the most difficult adjustment to master, but with practice, it produces some great results! If you're not confident in adjusting your curves graph from scratch, why not use a preset to get started? In step 2 on p. 42, select a preset from the **Curves** drop-down list.

 Save now! Click **File > Save As** and choose a new name for your file.

Which technique you choose depends on the photo you're working on. Other adjustments are covered in other tutorials and PhotoPlus Help topics. Experiment with different photos and adjustments and see what works for you.

Exporting your completed image to a common image file format will allow you to get full use from it. See *Saving & Exporting* on p. 187 for more information.

Sharpening Blurred Photos

 15 min

We've all found ourselves in the frustrating situation of discovering that a photo, which looked perfect on our digital camera's LCD screen, is blurry when we view it on the computer. Rather than throw the photo away, you can use PhotoPlus to add clarity or sharpen the image.

We'll show you several sharpening techniques, depending on the amount of blur the photo has.

By the end of this tutorial you will be able to:

- Create a duplicate layer and convert it to a filter layer.

- Apply a quick Clarity adjustment.

- Sharpen using High Pass filter with an Overlay blend mode.

- Use an Unsharp Mask filter.

Let's begin...

1.   On the Standard toolbar, click **Open**.

2.   Locate your chosen photo and click **Open**.

     The photo opens in the workspace.

Now we can explore a few techniques to help sharpen your photos—
beginning with a quick adjustment for slightly blurred images and then
moving on to more professional techniques for photos with a higher level
of blur.

> Some of the image adjustments made in this exercise can be applied directly
> to a photo, but for best practice we'll be using **adjustment layers** and **filter
> layers**.
>
> Adjustment layers and filter layers provide more flexibility and let you apply
> changes experimentally without affecting your original photo. You can turn
> these layers on and off to compare 'before' and 'after' states, and can easily
> edit and delete them later.

Duplicating a layer and converting to a filter layer

PhotoPlus makes it easy to duplicate a layer from the **Layers** tab and then
convert it to a filter layer.

To create a duplicate layer:

1.   On the **Layers** tab, right-click the **Background** layer, and select
     Duplicate.

2. In the **Duplicate Layer** dialog, accept the default settings and click OK.

   A duplicate layer, called **Background Copy**, is added to the Layers tab.

Now to convert it to a filter layer for maximum flexibility...

To convert a standard layer to a filter layer:

• On the **Layers** tab, right-click on the new **Background Copy** layer and click **Convert to Filter Layer**.

Now to look at clarity and sharpening.

Technique 1: Adjusting Clarity

The Clarity adjustment uses a contrast filter to quickly remove minor blur and softness from a photo—it may be all you need to improve your image.

This countryside scene has great composition, but the clarity of the tree foliage could be increased to improve the photo.

To apply a clarity adjustment:

1. With the **Background Copy** layer selected, from the **Image** menu, click **Adjust>Clarity**.

2. In the **Clarity** dialog, drag the slider to the right (or type a value) to increase the clarity of your photo.

    We increased the value to **50.0**.

3. Click **OK** to apply the adjustment.

As well as increased clarity in the tree foliage, you'll also notice the texture of the wool is much clearer.

 Save now! Click **File > Save As** and choose a new name for your file.

When saving, you may receive a warning message recommending you save your file as a PhotoPlus picture. Click **OK** to save as an .spp file so you can modify changes at a later date if necessary.

Technique 2: Sharpening using High Pass

At first the **High Pass** filter may only appear to be useful for creative, artistic effects. However, when combined with a layer blend mode, it's a highly customizable and effective way of sharpening blurred photos.

To add a High Pass filter:

1. With the **Background Copy** layer selected, from the **Effects** menu, click **Other>High Pass**.

2. In the **High Pass** dialog, drag the slider to the right (or type a value) to define the edges of your photo.

    We increased the value to **5.0**.

3. Click **OK** to apply the High Pass filter.

4.   On the **Layers** tab, from the blend mode drop-down list, select **Overlay**.

 Try experimenting by setting the blend mode to **Soft Light** or **Hard Light** to soften or strengthen the sharpening effect, respectively.

The definition in the fur has been enhanced using this technique.

Save now! Click **File** > **Save As** and choose a new name for your file.

Technique 3: Applying an Unsharp Mask

Unsharp Mask works mainly to enhance the edges in a photo. It's generally considered to be the standard tool for adjusting sharpness in photos. It's excellent for improving image quality, especially with scanned or resized pictures.

To apply an Unsharp Mask:

1. With the **Background Copy** layer selected, from the **Effects** menu, click **Sharpen**>Unsharp Mask.

2. In the **Unsharp Mask** dialog, drag the sliders (or type a value) to set the values.

    We set our values to:

    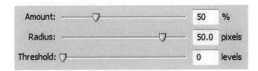

    - Amount: 50%

- **Radius:** 50.0

 For fine detail and/or low resolution images, use a lower radius setting (to avoid obliterating detail). Use higher settings with higher resolution photos.

- **Threshold:** 0

 Set the threshold too high and you'll see very little change in your photo. Generally, values between 0 and 5 are useful. Use a higher threshold for grainy images or skin tones (5 or sometimes more).

- Click **OK**.

Note especially the increase in depth and colour.

 Save now! Click **File > Save As** and choose a new name for your file.

Exporting your completed image to a common image file format will allow you to get full use from it. See *Saving & Exporting* on p. 187 for more information.

Combining Photos

 15-20 min

One advantage of digital cameras is the ability to take (almost) an unlimited amount of photos—in fact, you may find you frequently take several shots in quick succession to try and get the best out of a scene. What happens if you have almost identical scenes but like different sections from each? You can use PhotoPlus to combine them.

By the end of this tutorial you will be able to:

- Combine photos using a mask.

- Combine photos using the Clone tool.

In this tutorial, we will combine two photos of the moon.

Go to **http://go.serif.com/resources/HPX6** to download the following tutorial project file(s):

- moon.jpg
- moon_glow.jpg

Let's begin...

1.   On the Standard toolbar, click 📂 **Open**.

2.   Locate the **moon.jpg** file and click **Open**.

The photo opens in the workspace.

3.   Repeat the above steps to open **moon_glow.jpg**.

The second image opens in the workspace and both are displayed in the Documents tab.

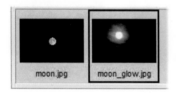

We are going to examine two methods of combining these photos to retain the detail from **moon.jpg** but the ethereal glow from **moon_glow.jpg**. We'll use a mask in the first instance and the Clone tool in the second. Let's get started.

Technique 1: Masking

Masks are discussed in detail in *Importance of Masks* in PhotoPlus Help, so let's dive right into the combining process.

To copy and paste as new layer:

1.   On the **Documents** tab, click to select **moon_glow.jpg**.

2.   From the **Edit** menu, click **Copy** (or press **Ctrl+C**).

3.   On the **Documents** tab, click to select **moon.jpg**.

4.   From the **Edit** menu, click **Paste>As New Layer** (or press **Ctrl+L**).

The copied photo is displayed in the workspace and added to the Layers tab as **Layer 1**.

With both photos now in the same project, the next step is to align them.

To align two photos:

1.   On the **Layers** tab:

•   Select **Layer 1** and reduce the **Opacity** to **60%**.

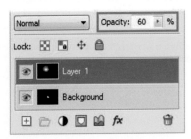

•   Select the **Background** layer.

2.   On the Tools toolbar, select the **Deform Tool**.

3. Drag the photo on the **Background** layer until the moon aligns with the central glow of **Layer 1**.

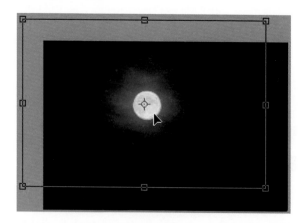

4. When you're happy with the positioning of the moon, on the **Layers** tab, increase the **Opacity** of **Layer 1** to **100%**.

With the photos now correctly aligned, we can begin revealing the moon on the Background layer through Layer 1.

 Save now! Click **File > Save As** and choose a new name for your file.

 When saving, you may receive a warning message recommending you save your file as a PhotoPlus picture. Click **OK** to save as an .spp file so you can modify changes at a later date if necessary.

To create a mask:

1. On the **Layers** tab, select **Layer 1** and then click 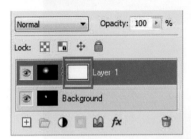 **Add Layer Mask**.

    A mask is added to Layer 1 and selected by default.

2. On the Tools toolbar, select the **Paintbrush Tool**.

3. On the **Brush Tip** tab, select **Basic** from the drop-down list, and then select the **32 pixel** soft brush.

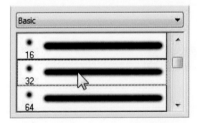

4. On the **Colour** tab, ensure the foreground colour is set to **black**.

5. Begin painting in the centre of the moon's glow, carefully moving out as you go.

You will notice the mask thumbnail on **Layer 1** (**Layers** tab) update as you paint.

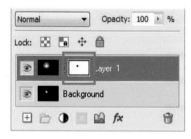

6. Continue painting until you are happy with the results.

 If you make a mistake along the way, on the **Colour** tab, switch the foreground colour to white and repaint over the mistake.

 As you get closer to the edge of the centre glow, reduce the **Size** and **Opacity** of your brush, using the context toolbar, to achieve a smooth blend.

You may be happy with this method of combining photos, but there may be occasions when this method just doesn't quite get the results you're looking for. A similar combined photo can be created using the Clone tool. We'll look at this method next.

 Don't forget to save your work!

Technique 2: Cloning

You'll first need to set up your PhotoPlus workspace as described in the *Let's begin* section on p. 54. and then display both photos side-by-side in the workspace.

To display open photos side-by-side:

*   From the **Window** menu, select **Tile Vertical**.

    Your photos are displayed side-by-side in the workspace.

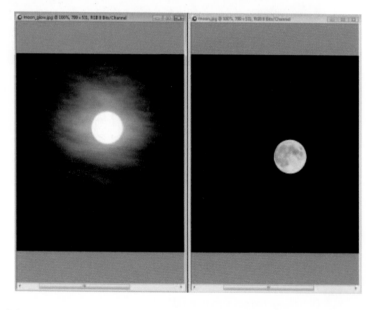

With both photos in view, the cloning becomes much easier.

You may also find it is useful to zoom into both photos and set up some guide lines to help you with the cloning process.

To adjust zoom level and add guides:

1. On the Standard toolbar, click the 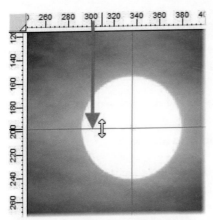 Zoom Tool and, from the context toolbar, select **Zoom All Windows**.

2. Click on your photo to zoom into the moon areas to the level you're comfortable with. We set ours to **400%**.

3. From the **View** menu, ensure **Rulers** is selected.

4. Click and drag from the side ruler to set up a vertical guide to bisect the moon.

5. Click and drag from the top ruler to set up a bisecting horizontal guide.

Once you have set the zoom and guides for both photos, we'll begin cloning.

It's good practice to clone onto a new layer so amendments can be easily made at a later date.

To add a new blank layer:

1. On the **Documents** tab, click to select **moon_glow.jpg**.

2. On the **Layers** tab, click ⊞ **New Layer** and, in the **Layer Properties** dialog, click **OK**.

    A new, transparent layer is added to the **Layers** tab.

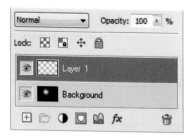

Now we can begin cloning!

Save now! Click **File** > **Save As** and choose a new name for your file.

To clone from one photo to another:

1. On the **Documents** tab, click to select **moon.jpg**.

2. On the **Tools** toolbar, select the 🔖 **Clone Tool** and then, on the context toolbar, ensure **Aligned** and **Use all layers** are selected.

3. On the **Brush Tip** tab, select **Basic** from the drop-down list, and then select the **32 pixel** soft brush.

4. Shift-click the centre of the moon to define the area to be cloned.

5. On the **Documents** tab, click to select **moon_glow.jpg**.

6. Begin painting in the centre of the moon's glow, carefully moving out as you go. As you paint, keep an eye on the area you are cloning from, marked with +.

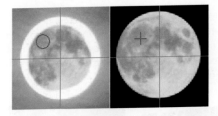

If you make a mistake along the way, on the Tools toolbar, select the 🖉 **Standard Eraser** and then erase your mistake. Then just switch back to the **Clone Tool** and continue cloning.

As you get closer to the edge of the centre glow, reduce the **Size** and **Opacity** of your brush, using the context toolbar, to achieve a smooth blend.

That's it! This resulting, combined photo looks stunning. Of course, you can always use both of these methods to combine a photo and give yourself maximum flexibility!

 Don't forget to save your work!

 Exporting your completed image to a common image file format will allow you to get full use from it. See *Saving & Exporting* on p. 187 for more information.

The techniques discussed in this tutorial would work equally well for group portraits (perhaps where someone is blinking in one photo but not in another) or landscapes (to eradicate distracting artefacts which move through a scene). It's particularly useful for getting a perfect picture of a popular, and busy, tourist attraction with no people in the way!

Sepia & Tinting

 15 min

Adding a tint can be a great way of being creative with your photos. However, it can also be a way of enhancing colour or correcting colour in photos. We'll explore several techniques for creating monochrome, tinted photos (looking in particular at sepia and rose tones) and using tints to enhance or correct photos.

By the end of this tutorial you will be able to:

• Convert a photo to sepia using an adjustment layer.

• Give a photo a rose tint using a layer Colour blend mode.

• Use a Lens Filter adjustment.

Let's begin...

1.   On the Standard toolbar, click 📂 **Open**.

2.   Locate your chosen photo and click **Open**.

    The photo opens in the workspace.

Converting photo to sepia

A quick way to convert a colour photo to sepia is to first convert it to black and white and then give it a sepia tint.

To add a Black and White Film adjustment:

1.   On the **Adjustments** tab, click **Black and White Film**.

    A Black and White Film adjustment layer is added.

    The Adjustments tab will update so you can make modifications to the Black and White Film adjustment.

2.   You can accept the default settings in the **Adjustments** tab, choose a preset from the **Black & White** drop-down list or customize the effect by dragging the colour sliders. We used the **Black Maximum** preset to emphasise the lamb.

Search *Black and White Film adjustment* in PhotoPlus Help for more information.

3.   On the **Adjustments** tab, with the **Black and White Film** adjustment still displayed, select the **Tint** check box.

The default settings give a soft sepia tint.

 Save now! Click **File > Save As** and choose a new name for your file.

When saving, you may receive a warning message recommending you save your file as a PhotoPlus picture. Click **OK** to save as an .spp file so you can modify changes at a later date if necessary.

Adding a rose tint using a Colour blend mode

Adding a tint using the layer Colour blend mode does not require a conversion to black and white first, and it can be tweaked at any time by just changing the fill layer colour.

To tint a photo using Blend Modes:

1.   On the **Layers** tab, click the  **New Fill or Adjustment Layer** and select **Fill Layer**.

2.   In the **Layer Properties** dialog, rename the layer 'Rose' and click **OK**.

3.   In the **Edit Fill** dialog, click the colour swatch.

4.   In the **Colour Selector** dialog, select a colour using the Hue slider and the Saturation and Lightness colour box (we selected H=0, S=100, L=86).

5.   Click **OK** twice to return to the workspace.

6.   On the **Layers** tab, set the blend mode to **Colour**.

Your photo immediately adopts your selected colour tint.

 Remember, you don't have to apply rose or sepia tints, you can apply any colour tint!

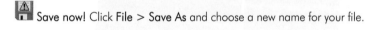 **Save now!** Click **File** > **Save As** and choose a new name for your file.

The two tinting methods previously described are more likely to be used as creative effects rather than photo adjustments. However, there will be times when you might want to add a tint to your photo to enhance it in a natural manner. To do this, you can use a Lens Filter adjustment.

Using a Lens Filter adjustment

The Lens Filter adjustment replicates the act of physically attaching a tinted filter to a camera's lens before a photo is taken. It's a great way of correcting colour or lighting issues with photos. The Lens Filter adjustment works particularly well to enhance the colours of sunsets.

To add a Lens Filter adjustment:

- On the **Adjustments** tab, click **Lens Filter**.

  By default, an orange lens filter is added to your photo.

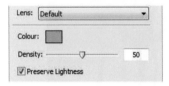

  This might be all you need to enhance a photo, such as a sunset scene.

Save now! Click **File > Save As** and choose a new name for your file.

If the default adjustment isn't appropriate for your photo, you can use one of the presets from the **Lens** drop-down list, or alternatively customize the adjustment to suit your needs.

We have two photos of the same leopard taken just minutes apart, however, the close-up photo suffers from poor lighting conditions which has given the photo a colder, blue tint.

We'll use the first photo to pick an appropriate colour to apply to our Lens Filter adjustment.

To customize a Lens Filter adjustment:

1. Open both photos as described at the beginning of this tutorial.

   Both photos are displayed in the Documents tab.

2. On the **Documents** tab, click to select the photo with the correct colour tint (in our case **Leopard.jpg**).

3. On the Tools toolbar, click the ✏ **Colour Pickup Tool** and then click on the photo to select a colour.

The Colour tab updates showing the picked colour as the foreground colour.

We'll use this as our Lens Filter colour.

4.   On the **Swatches** tab (if hidden, make this tab visible via **Window>Studio Tabs**), click ⬇ and choose **Add Category**, then type in a **Name** (e.g. Tinting) and click **OK**.

5.   With the new category selected, click ⊞ **Create Swatch.**

6.   On the **Documents** tab, click to select the photo you want to correct (in our case Leopard close.jpg).

7.   On the **Adjustments** tab, click **Lens Filter**, and then click the **Colour** swatch.

8.   In the **Colour Selector** dialog, click ▦ **Show swatches gallery** and from the category drop-down list, select your new category (e.g. Tinting).

9. In the gallery, click to select the newly added swatch and click **OK**.

Our photo has an improved, warm tint.

We can increase the richness of the photo's colour tint (to warm it further).

10. On the **Adjustments** tab, drag the **Density** slider to the right.

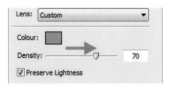

Our photo now has the perfect colour tone.

 Save now! Click **File** > **Save As** and choose a new name for your file.

Exporting your completed image to a common image file format will allow you to get full use from it. See *Saving & Exporting* on p. 187 for more information.

Makeup Makeover

 45 min

Some portrait photos can be greatly enhanced with the addition of a little makeup. With PhotoPlus, you can add this makeup after the photo shoot, giving you the flexibility to use the amount and colours you desire. Furthermore, you can experiment without wasting your model's precious time. So, for an easy digital makeover, take a look at the techniques below...

By the end of this tutorial you will be able to:

- Apply foundation and eyeshadow.

- Apply lipstick and gloss.

Go to **http://go.serif.com/resources/HPX6** to download the following tutorial project file(s):

makeup.jpg

Let's begin...

1.   On the Standard toolbar, click ⬚ **Open**.

2.   Locate your chosen photo and click **Open**.

     The photo opens in the workspace.

Foundation & eyeshadow

As with physical makeup, digital foundation can be applied to your model to give an even tone to their complexion and cover tiny flaws. You can also apply eyeshadow to enhance the eyes.

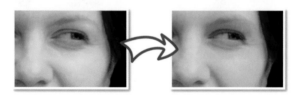

In PhotoPlus, the procedure for applying these makeups is similar, with little more than just the brush colour changing.

To apply foundation:

1.   On the **Layers** tab, click ⊞ **New Layer**.

2. In the **Layer Properties** dialog:

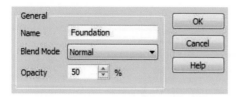

- Name your layer 'Foundation'.

- Set the **Opacity** to **50%**.

- Click **OK**.

  A new transparent layer is added to the Layers tab.

3. On the Tools toolbar, click the ✎ **Colour Pickup Tool** and, on the context toolbar, select **5 x 5 Average** from the **Sample Size** drop-down list.

  Hover over an area of skin tone to display a preview of the colour to be picked and click when you are happy with the displayed colour. This will become the foundation colour.

4.   On the Colour tab, the foreground colour is updated.

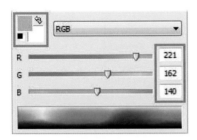

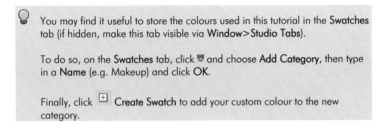

You may find it useful to store the colours used in this tutorial in the **Swatches** tab (if hidden, make this tab visible via **Window>Studio Tabs**).

To do so, on the **Swatches** tab, click ▽ and choose **Add Category**, then type in a **Name** (e.g. Makeup) and click **OK**.

Finally, click ⊞ **Create Swatch** to add your custom colour to the new category.

5.   On the Tools toolbar, click the 🖌 **Paintbrush Tool**.

6.   On the **Brush Tip** tab, select a brush tip (generally a soft-tipped brush from the **Basic** category is best).

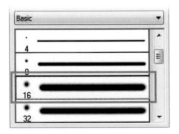

7. Paint over all areas of skin.

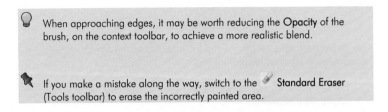

When approaching edges, it may be worth reducing the **Opacity** of the brush, on the context toolbar, to achieve a more realistic blend.

If you make a mistake along the way, switch to the ✎ **Standard Eraser** (Tools toolbar) to erase the incorrectly painted area.

8. If the current effect looks false, there are two ways to adjust the effect on the **Layers** tab:

* Reduce the **Opacity**.

* Change the blend mode to **Darken** or **Darken Colour**.

The model's skin should now appear flawless.

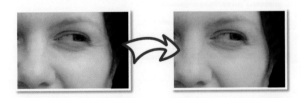

💾 **Save now!** Click **File > Save As** and choose a new name for your file.

When saving, you may receive a warning message recommending you save your file as a PhotoPlus picture. Click **OK** to save as an .spp file so you can modify changes at a later date if necessary.

Let's move onto eyeshadow. As the technique is so similar to applying foundation, we'll step through it quickly!

To apply eyeshadow:

1. On the **Layers** tab, click ⊞ New Layer.

2. In the **Layer Properties** dialog, name your layer 'Eyeshadow', set the **Opacity** to **50%** and click **OK**.

3. On the Standard toolbar, click the 🔍 **Zoom Tool** and then click on your image to zoom into the eye area.

4. On the Tools toolbar, click the ✎ **Paintbrush Tool**, and on the **Brush Tip** tab, select a soft brush tip.

5. On the **Colour** tab, use the sliders or colour box to select a colour for the eyeshadow.

Alternatively, use the ✎ **Colour Pickup Tool** to select a colour from your photo.

6.   Paint over the eyelids and, if desired, on the context toolbar, reduce the
Opacity to **50%** and paint the area under the eyebrows.

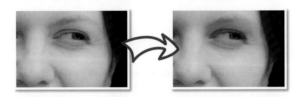

As before, feel free to adjust the blend mode and opacity on the **Layers**
tab to vary the effect.

Don't forget to save your work!

Lipstick & gloss

As with the other cosmetics we've already applied above, digital lipstick
does exactly the same as its physical counterpart—emphasize a model's
lips. We can also add a little gloss to make the lips shine and sparkle.
We'll go with a traditional red lipstick base, but feel free to experiment
with your own colours.

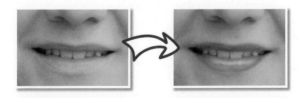

We're going to apply colour to the lips in four stages (lipstick, liner, gloss
and shine), using four separate layers, and to keep things neat within the
Layers tab (and to give you maximum control), you may wish to group
these layers.

To add a layer group:

*   On the **Layers** tab, click 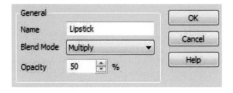 **New Layer Group**. Name the group 'Lips' and click **OK**.

    A new group is added to the Layers tab.

Now we can build up our layers within the Lips group.

To add lipstick:

1. On the **Layers** tab, with the **Lips** group still selected, click ⊞ **New Layer**.

2. In the **Layer Properties** dialog:

General		
Name	Lipstick	OK
Blend Mode	Multiply ▼	Cancel
Opacity	50 ▲▼ %	Help

    *   Name your layer 'Lipstick'.

    *   Set the blend mode to **Multiply**.

    *   Set the **Opacity** to **50%**.

    *   Click **OK**.

Your new layer is added to the group.

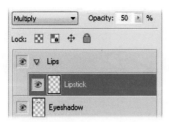

3. On the Standard toolbar, click the **Zoom Tool** and then click on your image to zoom into the lips area.

4. On the Tools toolbar, click the **Paintbrush Tool**.

5. On the **Brush Tip** tab, select a brush tip (generally a soft-tipped brush from the **Basic** category is best).

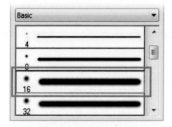

6. On the **Colour** tab, type directly into the RGB boxes to set the colour to R=195, G=78, B=62.

7. Paint over most of the lip area.

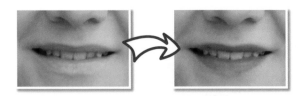

When approaching edges, it may be worth reducing the **Opacity** of the brush, on the context toolbar, to achieve a more realistic blend.

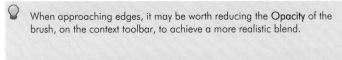

If you make a mistake along the way, switch to the ✏ **Standard Eraser** (Tools toolbar) to erase the incorrectly painted area.

To add lip liner:

1. Follow the steps 1-6 from *To add lipstick* on p. 82, with the following changes:

- Set the layer **Name** to 'Liner' and **Opacity** to **20%**.

- Set the brush **Colour** to R=144, G=12, B=0.

2. Paint across the lower edges of the upper and lower lips.

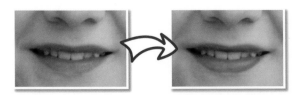

To add lip gloss:

1. Follow the steps 1-6 from *To add lipstick* on p. 82, with the following changes:

    - Set the layer **Name** to 'Gloss', the blend mode to **Soft Light** and **Opacity** to 70%.

    - Set the brush **Colour** to R=216, G=186, B=175.

2. Paint across the lips to add a little gloss.

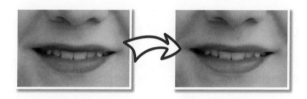

For a final touch, let's add some shine!

Don't forget to save your work!

To add shine:

1. On the **Layers** tab, click ⊞ **New Layer**.

2. In the **Layer Properties** dialog, name your layer 'Shine' and the **Opacity** to 50% and click **OK**.

Your new layer is added to the group.

3. On the Tools toolbar, click the ✏ **Paintbrush Tool**.

4. On the **Brush Tip** tab, from the category drop-down list, select **Media - Watercolour** and then select **Bristle Wet** (220 pix).

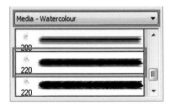

 Depending on the size of your photo, you may need to adjust the brush **Size** on the context toolbar—we set ours to 110.

5. On the **Colour** tab, click ✎ **Switch Colours** to set the foreground colour to white.

6. Click and drag across your photo to create a thick, glossy white line.

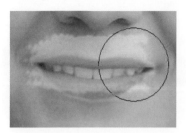

7. On the Tools toolbar, click the ⊹ **Move Tool**, and then drag the white line to position it so the lower edge runs across the middle of the bottom lip (as illustrated below).

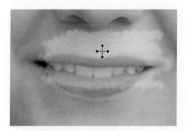

8. On the Tools toolbar, click ✎ **Standard Eraser**, and erase the line to leave a subtle shine to the lower lip and a tiny dab on the upper lip.

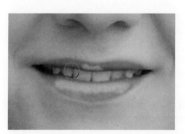

You can reduce the **Opacity** of the Standard Eraser from the context toolbar to create realistic blending.

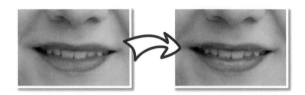

 To enhance the shine effect, you can repeat the above process to create a second **Shine** layer.

The lips on your model should now look fuller, richer and glossier. As we created the layers within a group, you can adjust the opacity of the group to vary the strength of the colour and shine.

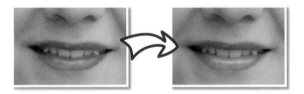

 Don't forget to save your work!

Feel free to experiment with these techniques to create more radical makeovers or to simulate other makeups.

If you've enjoyed this tutorial, why not check out the online *Retouching Portraits* video tutorials for more makeover techniques?

 Exporting your completed image to a common image file format will allow you to get full use from it. See *Saving & Exporting* on p. 187 for more information.

Creative Effects

You don't have to stick with realistic photo adjustments to get great results from your photo compositions. PhotoPlus has a variety of effects to help you get creative and produce photographic art like a professional. Take the opportunity to run wild with your creations or take a more subtle approach with these creative techniques.

Selective Colour Effect

 5-10 min

Have you ever seen black and white photos with an isolated area of the photo appearing in colour? The technique is known as selective colour, colour popping or spot colour. It can be an effective way of drawing the viewer's attention to the key focal points in the frame. The best part is that in PhotoPlus this is really easy to do—we'll show you how.

By the end of this tutorial you will be able to:

- Convert a photograph to black and white using a Channel Mixer adjustment.

- Create a colour pop effect by modifying a mask.

 For more information about masking, search *Importance of Masks* in PhotoPlus Help.

You can easily use any photo for this technique, but we've also provided the tutorial file for you to use.

 Go to **http://go.serif.com/resources/HPX6** to download the following tutorial project file(s):

⊙ guitar.jpg

Let's begin...

1.   On the Standard toolbar, click  Open.

2.   Locate the **guitar.jpg** (or your own photo) and click **Open**.

The photo opens in the workspace.

Converting to black and white

As this is a colour photo, the first thing we need to do is apply an adjustment layer to allow us to create a black and white image while retaining the RGB channels.

To add a Channel Mixer adjustment:

1.   On the **Adjustments** tab, click **Channel Mixer**.

A new adjustment layer is added to the Layers tab.

2.   On the **Adjustments** tab, from the **Channel Mixer** drop-down list, select **Monochrome (Green)**.

The **Output Channel** and **Source Channels** update to display the settings of the selected preset.

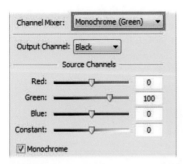

Now we have an ideal high contrast black and white photo, let's expose some colour!

 Save now! Click **File > Save As** and choose a new name for your file.

 When saving, you may receive a warning message recommending you save your file as a PhotoPlus picture. Click **OK** to save as an .spp file so you can modify changes at a later date if necessary.

Using a mask

To create the selective colour effect, we need to reveal some of the
original photo. When you add an adjustment layer, a mask is
automatically created for that layer (notice the white thumbnail).

All we need to do is paint on the mask to reveal the layer beneath. Let's
do this now.

To reveal colour:

1.   On the **Layers** tab, click to select the white mask thumbnail.

2.   On the **Colour** tab, click ■ **Reset Colours**. The foreground swatch is set
to black while the background swatch is set to white.

3.   On the Tools toolbar, click the ✎ **Paintbrush Tool**.

4.   On the **Brush Tip** tab, from the category drop-down list, select **Basic**
and then choose an appropriate size soft brush tip. (We chose a **64**
pixel brush.)

5.   Start painting around the body of the guitar.

Notice that, as black is painted on the mask, the colour from the layer beneath is revealed.

Don't worry about being too accurate with the paintbrush at this stage—we can easily fix any mistakes in the next step.

6. To paint inside the tricky areas, either select a smaller brush tip from the **Brush Tip** tab, or reduce the size using the context toolbar.

When you've finished painting on the mask, you should have an image similar to ours.

Notice that there are some areas of colour that we don't want revealed (such as on the hands and the shirt). Let's fix this now.

7. On the **Colour** tab, click ✎ **Switch Colours**. The foreground swatch is set to white while the background swatch is set to black.

8.   Paint over the areas where you want to hide the colour again. (Use the
      🔍 **Zoom Tool** to zoom in if you need to.)

Once you've finished tidying up the masked areas, your selective colour
effect is complete!

 Don't forget to save your work!

Why not colour pop from a sepia background or a reduced vibrance
photo (see *Sepia & Tinting* on p. 65 and *Key Adjustments: Vibrance* on
p. 37)? Have fun!

If you've enjoyed this tutorial, we use similar masking technique can be
used to create a *Depth of Field Effect* on p. 105—why not check it out?

🖈   Exporting your completed image to a common image file format will allow
     you to get full use from it. See *Saving & Exporting* on p. 187 for more
     information.

Tilt-Shift Miniature Effect

10 min

A Tilt-Shift effect gives the illusion of photographing a miniature (or model) by having a band of sharp focus sandwiched between two bands of heavy blur. The **Depth of Field** effect in PhotoPlus is perfect for applying a Tilt-Shift Miniature effect to your photos.

It can be difficult to find a photo which works well as a miniature—the photo must be taken at a relatively high angle and contain an area which has a clear subject. The photo will usually include buildings, landscapes or vehicles.

We've provided a great photo for you to use in this tutorial, so you can get started straightaway.

By the end of this tutorial you will be able to:

- Add a duplicate, filter layer for flexible working.

- Apply a Tilt-Shift (Depth of Field) effect.

    Go to **http://go.serif.com/resources/HPX6** to download the following tutorial project file(s):

🔾 castle.jpg

Let's begin...

1. On the Standard toolbar, click 🗁 **Open**.

2. Locate your chosen photo and click **Open**.

   The photo opens in the workspace.

Before we apply the Tilt-Shift effect to the photo, we'll create a duplicate layer and then convert it to a filter layer. This will give us flexibility if we wish to modify the effect at a later date.

Create a duplicate, filter layer

By duplicating your background layer, you are retaining the original within the project to refer back to while you work. You can also revert back to the original at any time.

To create a duplicate layer:

1. On the **Layers** tab, right-click the **Background** layer, and select **Duplicate**.

2. In the **Duplicate Layer** dialog, rename the layer as 'Tilt-Shift' and click OK.

   A duplicate layer is added to the Layers tab.

The Tilt-Shift effect can be applied directly to this new duplicate layer, however, we'll convert it to a filter layer first so we can modify the effect at a later date.

To convert to a filter layer:

- On the **Layers** tab, right-click the **Tilt-Shift** layer, and select **Convert to Filter Layer**.

Now let's look at applying the effect!

 Save now! Click **File** > **Save As** and choose a new name for your file.

 When saving, you may receive a warning message recommending you save your file as a PhotoPlus picture. Click **OK** to save as an .spp file so you can modify changes at a later date if necessary.

Applying a Tilt-Shift effect

The Depth of Field blur effect can be used to create the contrasting in-focus and out of focus areas necessary to give the illusion of a photographed miniature.

To add a filter effect:

1. On the **Layers** tab, select the **Tilt-Shift** layer.

2. From the **Effects** menu, click **Blur>Depth of Field**.

3. In the dialog, from the **Type** drop-down list, select **Tilt-Shift**.

    The workspace displays your photo with a preview of the effect, including adjustable lines and nodes.

A - Focal Point, B - Depth of Field (i.e. the in-focus region), C - Transitional Region, D - Blurred Region (i.e. the out of focus region)

 For more information on the Tilt-Shift lines and nodes and how to adjust them, search *Adjusting Depth of Field effects* in PhotoPlus Help.

We'll tweak the default settings to get the effect looking precisely how we want.

To edit the filter effect:

1. We want the focus to be on the duel in the roped arena, but specifically to ensure the swordsman on the right remains in focus. The default settings place the area of focus in our photo slightly too high—we'll adjust this first.

    On the preview, click and drag the central **focal point** downwards so the swordsman on the right stands exactly between the **depth of field** lines.

2. The crowd in the background still remains partly in focus—we'll extended the area of transition to blur them more. The area of focus will also become narrower.

On the preview, click and drag the upper **transitional region** line downwards until the background crowd becomes blurred.

To really get that miniaturized effect, we need to boost the brightness (to emphasize the bokeh effect) and colour of the photo.

We'll do that next.

To boost brightness (bokeh) and colour:

1. Back in the dialog, in the **Boost** section, set the following:

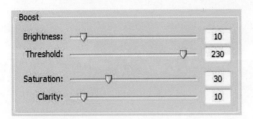

*   **Brightness** to 10—this determines the brightness of the blurred pixels (emphasize the bokeh effect).

*   **Threshold** to 230—this determines which blurred pixels are affected by the Brightness setting (the higher the number, the fewer pixels affected).

*   **Saturation** to 30—this boosts the photo's colour.

*   **Clarity** to 10—restores some of the sharpness of the photo lost by the other Boost settings.

2. When you're happy with the results in the preview, click **OK**.

    The Depth of Field filter effect is added to the Layers tab...

...and applied to the photo.

 Don't forget to save your work!

 Exporting your completed image to a common image file format will allow you to get full use from it. See *Saving & Exporting* on p. 187 for more information.

Depth of Field Effect

🕐 15 min ✏️ ✏️ ✏️ ✏️ ✏️

Depth of field describes the distance between the nearest and farthest points in a photo which are in focus. Small depths of field can be effective for emphasizing a foreground or background subject. Photos taken with a large depth of field, i.e. where the entire photo appears sharp, can be altered in PhotoPlus to using a depth of field effect.

By the end of this tutorial you will be able to:

• Use the Clone tool to prepare the photo for blurring.

• Convert a standard layer to a filter layer.

• Apply a Depth of Field filter effect.

• Apply and adjust a mask to enhance the depth of field effect.

You can easily use any photo for this technique, but we've also provided the tutorial file for you to use.

⬇️ Go to **http://go.serif.com/resources/HPX6** to download the following tutorial project file(s):

🔸 sculpture.jpg

Let's begin...

1. On the Standard toolbar, click  **Open**.

2. Locate your chosen photo and click **Open**.

The photo opens in the workspace.

Cloning onto a duplicate layer

To create our depth of field we need two layers—one which is sharp and in focus (which contains our subject) and a second which is blurred and out of focus (which contains the distracting clutter). The layers need to be identical to begin with, so we'll create a duplicate layer...

To create a duplicate layer:

1. On the **Layers** tab, right-click the **Background** layer, and select **Duplicate**.

2. In the **Duplicate Layer** dialog, rename the layer as 'Blurred' and click OK.

A duplicate layer is added to the Layers tab.

To avoid confusion later on, you may also wish to rename the Background layer to something more appropriate.

To rename a layer:

1. On the **Layers** tab, double-click the **Background** layer.

2. In the **Layer Properties** dialog, type in a new name, such as 'Focus', and click **OK**.

To create the Depth of Field effect we'll apply a blur to the Blurred layer and then mask it to reveal the Focus layer underneath. If we do this immediately, the results would include a nasty halo (see below).

To avoid this halo, we can extend the hills and sky over the sculpture on the Blurred layer using the Clone tool.

To clone the background:

1.   On the Tools toolbar, click the ⚓ **Clone Tool** and on the context toolbar, ensure the **Aligned** option is selected (so that each new stroke lines up with the previous one).

2.   On the **Brush Tip** tab, from the category drop-down list, select **Basic** and then choose **Round07** (64 pixel width).

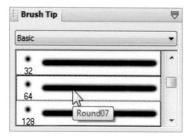

3.   **Shift**-click on the area of green foliage just to the right of the sculpture, just above the fence line. This defines the clone source for the new area.

4. With the **Blurred** layer selected, click and drag along the right-hand edge of the sculpture until you get to the top of the head. Don't worry about being too neat.

5. Repeat steps 3 and 4, except this time select a source in the foliage to the left of the sculpture.

    The image should now resemble the example below—don't worry if it looks a little strange at this point!

 For more information on using the Clone tool, search *Cloning a region* in PhotoPlus Help.

Now we can begin building up the depth of field effect...

 Save now! Click **File** > **Save As** and choose a new name for your file.

 When saving, you may receive a warning message recommending you save your file as a PhotoPlus picture. Click **OK** to save as an .spp file so you can modify changes at a later date if necessary.

Adding blur

Before we proceed any further, we're going to convert the Blurred layer to a filter layer. This will allow us to modify the blur after it has been applied, if we're not happy with the later results.

To convert to a filter layer:

- On the **Layers** tab, right-click the **Blurred** layer, and select **Convert to Filter Layer**.

With our layers set up, we'll blur the Blurred layer using a Depth of Field filter effect.

To add a filter effect:

1. On the **Layers** tab, select the **Blurred** layer.

2. From the **Effects** menu, click **Blur>Depth of Field**.

The workspace displays your photo with a preview of the effect.

3. In the dialog, from the **Type** drop-down list, select **Linear Gradient**.

The preview's depth of field lines and nodes update to represent a linear gradient.

A - Focal Point, B - Depth of Field (i.e. the in-focus region), C - Transitional Region, D - Blurred Region (i.e. the out of focus region)

 For more information on the Depth of Field lines and nodes and how to adjust them, search *Adjusting Depth of Field effect* in PhotoPlus Help.

We'll tweak the default settings to get the effect looking precisely how we want.

To edit the filter effect:

1. We want the depth of field (in-focus) region to lie across the base of the sculpture. The default settings place the area of focus in our photo far too high.

    On the preview, click and drag the **depth of field** line downwards until the **focal point** is located at the sculpture's base.

2. In the dialog, click **OK** to apply the effect.

    The Depth of Field filter effect is added to the Layers tab...

...and applied to the photo.

As you can see, the Depth of Field blurs everything from the base of the sculpture upwards. However, the entire sculpture should really be in focus. We can regain the sculpture's sharpness using a layer mask.

 Don't forget to save your work!

Adding and adjusting a layer mask

By adding a mask to the Blurred layer, we can selectively reveal the Focus layer underneath and therefore bring the sculpture back into focus. Let's do that now.

 For more information on using masks, search *Importance of Masks* in PhotoPlus Help.

To add a mask:

• On the **Layers** tab, with the **Blurred** layer selected, click  **Add Layer Mask**.

A mask is added to the layer and selected by default (as indicated with the thumbnail's white border).

Now we need to edit the mask...

To edit a mask:

1. On the Tools toolbar, click the **Paintbrush Tool**.

2. On the **Brush Tip** tab, select a brush tip (generally a soft-tipped brush from the **Basic** category is best).

3. On the **Colour** tab, click ■ **Reset Colours** to set the foreground swatch to black.

4. Paint over the photo to reveal the in-focus sculpture.

When the sculpture has been fully revealed, you might discover areas where the mask has extended too far and the background has come into focus.

We'll resolve this now.

To tidy up the effect:

1. On the context toolbar, reduce the **Size** of the brush.

2. On the **Colour** tab, click ⚅ **Switch Colours** to set the foreground swatch to white.

3. Paint over the in-focus areas you wish to blur again.

4. If you make a mistake along the way, on the **Colour** tab, switch the foreground colour back to black and repaint over the mistake.

That's it! The depth of field effect is complete.

Tilt-Shift is another photo lens effect you can create using PhotoPlus's Depth of Field effect, see *Tilt-Shift Miniature Effect* on p. 97 for more information.

 Don't forget to save your work!

 Exporting your completed image to a common image file format will allow you to get full use from it. See *Saving & Exporting* on p. 187 for more information.

1970s Retro Effect

 15-20 min

Due to the chemicals used for processing, many photos from the 1970s have since deteriorated. This deterioration has made the 1970s look fashionable and you can use PhotoPlus to convert your digital photo into a retro picture for a variety of purposes.

By the end of this tutorial you will be able to:

- Crop a photo to remove modern features.

- Add and edit Levels and Curves adjustments.

- Adjust layer blend range.

- Add a vignette and add noise.

In the following exercise, we've taken a recent photo of a motorcyclist riding a classic bike, and given the impression it was taken and developed in the 1970s. You can try this with a variety of your own photos or you can use the one that we have provided.

Go to http://go.serif.com/resources/HPX6 to download the following tutorial project file(s):

○ motorbike.jpg

Let's begin...

1. On the Standard toolbar, click 🗀 **Open**.

2. Locate the **motorbike.jpg** (or your own photo) and click **Open**.

The photo opens in the workspace.

Cropping photo

Our photo contains some background elements which could potentially ruin the aging effect we are going to apply—such as the modern clothing of the spectators. We'll use a standard print size crop to remove the background spectators.

See *Learning to Crop* on p. 25 for more information about cropping.

To add a crop:.

1. On the Tools toolbar, select the ⬜ **Crop Tool**.

2. On the context toolbar, in the left-most drop-down list, choose a pre-defined print size. We chose 6 x 4 in.

3. Drag out to define your crop selection area.

4. Double-click inside the crop selection to crop to the designated size. The print resolution adjusts to honour the print dimensions.

Adjusting levels

To begin the retro effect, we'll adjust the levels to give the photo a faded, bleached look. If you are using your own photo, you may wish to experiment with the settings listed below.

See Key Adjustments: Adjusting Levels on p. 39 for more information about Levels adjustments.

To adjust levels:

1. On the **Adjustments** tab, click **Levels**.

   A new adjustment layer is added.

2. On the **Adjustments** tab, drag the grey arrow to the left to place the midtones at 1.5.

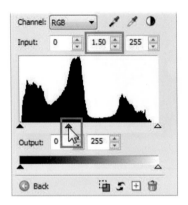

3. From the **Channels** drop-down list, select the **Red** channel and then set the following levels:

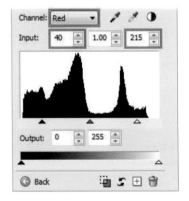

- Set the black input to **40**.

- Set the white input to **215**.

4. From the **Channels** drop-down list, select the **Blue** channel and then set midtones to **0.5**.

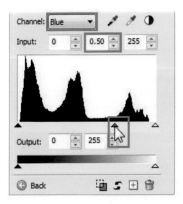

Our photo now has an aged look, but the aging is too consistent across the photo to be authentic.

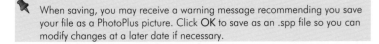

Save now! Click **File > Save As** and choose a new name for your file.

When saving, you may receive a warning message recommending you save your file as a PhotoPlus picture. Click **OK** to save as an .spp file so you can modify changes at a later date if necessary.

Reducing layer blend range

PhotoPlus allows you to reduce the range over which a layer blends with the layer below. This is controlled in the Layer Properties dialog. We'll use this feature to give the photo a more authentic faded appearance.

To adjust a layer's blend range:

1. On the **Layers** tab, right-click the **Levels** layer and select **Properties**.

    The **Layer Properties** dialog will open.

    Moving the Underlaying Layer arrows will cause areas of the layer below (i.e. the Background layer) to show through the current Levels layer. The white arrow affects the lightest areas in the photo, and the black arrow affects the darkest areas.

    Search *Using blend ranges* in PhotoPlus Help for more information.

2. In the **Blend Ranges** section, drag the **Underlying Layer** black arrow to the right to set the black range to **94/94**.

The darkest areas of the **Background** layer will begin showing through, but the effect is too stark.

3. Press the **Alt** key and then drag the **Underlying Layer** black arrow to the right once more. The arrow will split into two, allowing a smooth transition between the two layers in the new range selected.

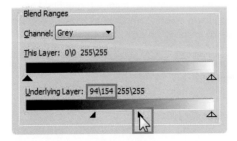

Set the black range to **94/154**.

4. Click **OK** to set the layer blend range.

Now the aging looks more realistic.

Photos from the 1970s sometimes display incorrect colour tones. This is because some of the chemicals used in processing photos in the 1970s have become unstable. In general, the blue dyes have broken down more, leaving photos with a red-yellow tint. We'll replicate this next.

 Don't forget to save your work!

Adjusting curves

The Curves adjustment lets you correct the tonal range of a photo—the spread of lightness values through shadow, midtone, and highlight regions—and control individual colour components. However, it can also be used to creative effect by creating an aged tonal effect.

See *Key Adjustments: Adjusting Curves* on p. 42 for more information about Curves adjustments.

To apply a curves adjustment:

1. On the **Adjustments** tab, if the Levels adjustment is still displayed, click
    ◉ **Back** and then click **Curves**.

    A new adjustment layer is added.

2. From the **Channels** drop-down list, select the **Red** channel and then click and drag the **Curves** graph upwards to increase the overall red tint (as shown below).

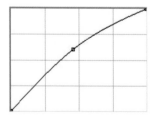

3. From the **Channels** drop-down list, select the **Blue** channel and then click and drag the **Curves** graph downwards to decrease the overall blue tint.

    Also, drag the left and right points toward the centre of the graph to reduce blue from the shadows and highlights (as shown below).

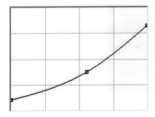

    The colour tint firmly places the photo in the 1970s, but the effect is too vivid.

4. On the **Layers** tab, select the **Curves** layer and reduce the **Opacity** to 80%.

The tint is now slight softer, adding to the retro photo's authenticity.

 Don't forget to save your work!

Adding a vignette

To continue adding to the retro effect, we can add a vignette.

> Vignetting is the appearance of areas of brighter or darker contrast at the corners or edges of a photo. There are several ways in which a vignette can be caused, including the mechanics of older cameras. Most modern cameras will automatic adjust settings to avoid creating vignettes, but they can now be added after processing to great creative effect.

To add a vignette:

1. On the **Layers** tab, click the ◑ **New Fill or Adjustment Layer** and select **Fill Layer**.

2. In the **Layer Properties** dialog:

- Rename the layer 'Vignette'.

- Set the **Blend Mode** to **Soft Light**.

- Set the **Opacity** to **20%**.

- Click **OK**.

3. In the **Edit Fill** dialog, from the **Fill Type** drop-down list, click **Radial**, and then select the **Reverse** option so the gradient runs from white to black.

4. Click **OK**.

A soft vignette effect is added to your photo.

 Don't forget to save your work!

Adding noise

A 'fast film', used for photographing high-speed motion, might have been used in a camera to capture this picture in the 1970s. High-speed film frequently resulted in a grainy images. We can fake this grain by adding noise to our photo.

To add noise:

1. On the **Layers** tab, right-click the **Background** layer and select Duplicate.

2. In the **Duplicate Layer** dialog, type 'Noise' in the **As** text input box and click **OK**.

    Your new, duplicate layer is added to the Layers tab.

3. Right-click this new layer and select **Convert to Filter Layer**.

4. From the **Effects** menu, click **Noise** and then select **Add Noise**.

5. In the **Add Noise** dialog, drag the slider to set the **Percentage** to 4, and click **OK**.

This subtle grain gives your photo that finishing touch—your retro photo is now complete!

 Don't forget to save your work!

 Exporting your completed image to a common image file format will allow you to get full use from it. See *Saving & Exporting* on p. 187 for more information.

Typographic Portrait Effect

🕐 30-45 min ✏️✏️✏️✏️✏️

Typographic portraits are images which are made entirely of text.

The words, font and text size used to create the typographic portrait can have a strong impact on the image and can create either a fun or compelling atmosphere.

By the end of this tutorial you will be able to:

• Create a custom text brush.

• Create a mask using a photo's shadows and midtones.

• Use the Paintbrush Tool in conjunction with a custom brush to add text.

• Apply a layer mask from a predefined image.

We've provided our custom brush project file for you to use in this tutorial, should you wish to save time.

⬇️ Go to **http://go.serif.com/resources/HPX6** to download the following tutorial project file(s):

🔘 text_brush.spp

Let's begin...

Rather than break up the creative process, we'll create our custom text brush now to use later in this tutorial. If, instead, you want to skip this process, simply download the provided file and add the brush to the **Brush Tips** tab as described in *To convert a text image to a brush* on p. 134.

To create a new document:

1. On the **File** menu, click **New**.

2. In the **New Image** dialog:

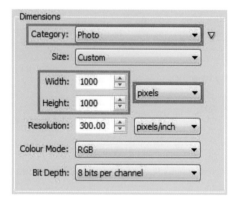

*   Set the **Category** to Photo.

*   Set the measurement units to **pixels**.

*   Set the size to **1000 x 1000**.

*   Click **OK**.

    A new blank document opens.

Creating a custom brush

Creating a custom brush can be as simple as importing, or copying, your open image to the Brush Tip tab. For details search *Creating your own brush tips* in PhotoPlus Help. We'll use the Text Tool to build up the words for the text brush and then add it to the Brush Tip tab.

To add text to an image:

1. On the Tools toolbar, from the Text Tools flyout, select the **T** Text Tool.

2. Click and drag on your image to add a text insertion point.

   When you release the mouse button, a text insertion point appears and a new text layer is added to the Layers tab.

3. On the context toolbar, set the font, size and format as required. We set our font to **Georgia**.

4. Type your word.

5.   Repeat steps 2-4 to add more words to your image (and text layers to the Layers tab), until you are happy with the image.

6.   (Optional) On the Tools toolbar, select the **⊹ Move Tool**, and drag to adjust the position of your words.

Your text image should now have a similar feel to the example below:

 The above image (**text_brush.spp**) is available for download (see p. 131).

Now to convert this to a brush...

Save now! Click **File > Save As** and choose a new name for your file.

To convert a text image to a brush:

1.   On the **Brush Tip** tab, right-click on the brush gallery and select **Add Category**.

2.   In the **Category** dialog, rename the category (e.g. 'Text') and click **OK**.

3.   On the Tools toolbar, select the ⬚ **Rectangle Selection Tool** and drag a selection box around your text image.

4. On the **Brush Tip** tab, right-click on the **Text** category gallery and select **Define Brush**.

5. In the **New Brush** dialog, rename the brush (e.g. 'Text') and click **OK**.

The new brush is added to the Brush Tip tab.

6. On the **Brush Tip** tab, right-click the newly created brush and select **Brush Options**.

7. In the **Brush Options** dialog, from the **Attributes** section, select **Spacing** and then increase the **Spacing** to 120.

This will ensure that, when you use the brush, you will add the text sparingly and not saturate your typographic portrait.

8. Click **OK** to exit the dialog and update the brush settings.

With our text brush ready to use, let's create our typographic portrait!

Creating a mask from shadows and midtones

A typographic portrait can be constructed by filling in midtones and shadows with text and leaving highlights as contrasting areas of white. Before we do this, we need to open a photo.

To open a photo:

1. On the Standard toolbar, click 🖾 **Open**.

2. Locate your chosen photo and click **Open**.

The photo opens in the workspace.

Now we need to define the areas we want filled with text, starting with the shadows.

To define shadows:

1. From the **Select** menu, click **Colour Range**.

2. In the **Colour Range** dialog, from the **Select** drop-down list, click **Shadows**.

 To preview the selection, select the **Show Selection** option.

3. Click **OK**.

    All the shadows in your photo are selected.

4. From the **Edit** menu, select **Copy** (or press **Ctrl+C**).

5. From the **Edit** menu, select **Paste>As New Layer** (or press **Ctrl+L**).

You will now have a new layer dedicated to the shadows in your photo.

6. From the **Select** menu, click **Deselect** (or press **Ctrl+D**).

Now we'll repeat the process to define the midtones in the photo.

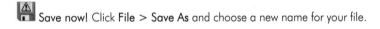 Save now! Click **File** > **Save As** and choose a new name for your file.

 When saving, you may receive a warning message recommending you save your file as a PhotoPlus picture. Click **OK** to save as an .spp file so you can modify changes at a later date if necessary.

To define midtones:

1. On the **Layers** tab, select the **Background** layer.

2. From the **Select** menu, click **Colour Range**.

3. In the **Colour Range** dialog, from the **Select** drop-down list, click **Midtones** and then click **OK**.

The midtones in your photo are selected.

4. From the **Edit** menu, select **Copy** (or press **Ctrl+C**).

5. From the **Edit** menu, select **Paste>As New Layer** (or press **Ctrl+L**).

You will now have a two layers, one dedicated to shadows (Layer 1) and another to midtones (Layer 2).

6. From the **Select** menu, click **Deselect** (or press **Ctrl+D**).

These two new layers will eventually be used to create a layer mask and therefore they need to be a shade of grey. For details on masks, search *Importance of Masks* in PhotoPlus Help.

Don't forget to save your work!

To convert a layer to black and white (greyscale):

1. On the **Layers** tab, select the midtones layer.

2. From the **Edit** menu, click **Fill**.

3. In the **Fill** dialog:

- Select **Custom**.

- Click the **Custom** swatch and in the **Colour Selector** dialog, in the **H**, **S** and **L** input boxes, type '0', '0', and '50', respectively (i.e. HSL=0, 0, 50) then click **OK**.

- Ensure **Preserve Transparency** option is selected.

- Click **OK**.

    The midtone layer is converted to 50% grey while retaining each pixel's transparency level.

4. On the **Layers** tab, select the shadows layer and repeat the steps above but define the custom colour as **HSL=0, 0, 0** (i.e. black).

    The shadows layer is converted to black while retaining each pixel's transparency level.

Now we'll merge these layers together...

 Don't forget to save your work!

To merge layers:

1. On the **Layers** tab, hold down the **Shift** key and click to select both midtones and shadow layers, then right-click and select **Merge Selected Layers**.

2. On the **Layers** tab, double-click the merged layer and, in the **Layer Properties** dialog, rename the layer 'Mask' and click **OK**.

   Your mask is now ready for later use.

Next we'll begin painting our text.

 Don't forget to save your work!

Painting using a text brush

We'll use the Paintbrush Tool to build up text on your image, but first we'll set up the layers to work on.

To add a new fill layer:

1. On the **Layers** tab, select the **Background** layer and then click the ◑ **New Fill or Adjustment Layer** and select **Fill Layer**.

2. In the **Layer Properties** dialog, click **OK** to accept the default settings.

3. In the **Edit Fill** dialog, click the colour swatch.

4. In the **Colour Selector** dialog, in the H, S and L input boxes, type '0', '0', and '100', respectively (i.e. HSL=0, 0, 100).

5. Click **OK** twice to return to the workspace.

6. On the **Layers** tab, select the **Mask** layer and click ⊞ **New Layer**.

7. In the **Layer Properties** dialog, rename the layer 'Words' and click **OK**.

    Your new layers are displayed on the Layers tab.

Now to add our text...

To paint text:

1. With the **Words** layer selected, on the Tools toolbar, from the Brush Tools flyout, select the ✐ **Paintbrush Tool**.

2. On the **Brush Tips** tab, from the category drop-down list, select **Text** and then click your custom **Text** brush.

3. On the **Colour** tab, click ■ **Reset Colours** to set the foreground swatch to black.

4. Click and drag with your brush to paint text onto your photo.

Now we'll apply a mask to the Words layer using the midtones and shadows defined on the Mask layer.

Don't forget to save your work!

Applying a mask

We'll use the previously created midtones and shadows image on the Mask layer to create a mask for the Words layer. Although this sounds complicated, it is quite straightforward—just follow the steps carefully.

To add a mask from a selection:

1. On the **Layers** tab, select the **Mask** layer.

2. From the **Select** menu, click **Select All** (or press **Ctrl+A**).

3. From the **Edit** menu, select **Copy** (or press **Ctrl+C**).

4. On the **Layers** tab, select the **Words** layer and click Add Layer Mask.

    A reveal all mask is added to the Words layer.

5. On the **Layers** tab, press the **Alt** key and click the mask thumbnail.

This will display only the mask in the main workspace.

6. With the selection still in place, from the **Edit** menu, select
Paste>Into Selection (or press **Ctrl+Shift+L**).

The image from the Mask layer is now pasted on the Words layer's
mask.

7. From the **Select** menu, click **Deselect** (or press **Ctrl+D**).

8. From the **Image** menu, click **Adjust>Negative Image** to invert your
mask.

All the black areas will hide the text on the layer, while the white
areas will enable the text to show through. For more information on
masks, search *Importance of Masks* in PhotoPlus Help.

9. Finally, on the **Layers** tab, select the **Mask** layer and drag it below
Layer 1.

Your typographic portrait is beginning to take form, but we need to pull the photo out more.

 Don't forget to save your work!

Redefining the photo

Due to the lack of paint on the Words layer, we have lost much of the original photo's detail. We can bring this back by continuing to paint on the Words layer using our custom text brush. If we vary the size and opacity, we can achieve a lovely typographic effect.

To paint to redefine lines:

1. On the **Layers** tab, select the **Words** layer.

    The Paintbrush Tool should still be selected and set to your custom Text brush tip and a black colour, if not, reselect these options.

2. On the context toolbar, reduce the brush **Size** to **500** and the **Opacity** to 75%.

3. Click and drag with your brush to paint text onto your photo.

4. On the context toolbar, reduce the brush **Size** to **100** and the **Opacity** to **50%** and continue to paint to define strong facial features, such as eyes, nose, ears, lips and chin.

5. Next, on the **Brush Tip** tab, select a soft tip brush from the **Basic** category, and reduce the **Opacity**, on the context toolbar, to **30%**.

6. Continue to paint around the facial features and hair of your portrait model for additional emphasis.

Now we have refined the edges of the photo, our typographic portrait effect is complete!

Why not experiment with other photos and other custom text brushes?

 If you've enjoyed this tutorial and are interested in find out more uses for text and custom brushes, see *Copyrights & Captions* on p. 177.

 Don't forget to save your work!

 Exporting your completed image to a common image file format will allow you to get full use from it. See *Saving & Exporting* on p. 187 for more information.

Watercolour Effect

 30 min

A great way of transforming your photos, particularly if they are a little out of focus or blurry, is creating a piece of artwork from them. We're going to take a slightly blurred photo of a lamb in a field and transform it into a realistic watercolour.

By the end of this tutorial you will be able to:

- Apply an effect from the Filter Gallery.

- Apply an effect from the Effects menu.

- Add a pattern to give the illusion of texture.

- Use Clip to Layer to isolate an adjustment layer.

- Promote a layer and create a layer group.

- Create a border by painting a mask.

Go to **http://go.serif.com/resources/HPX6** to download the following tutorial project file(s):

◉ lamb.jpg

Let's begin...

- On the Standard toolbar, click 🗁 **Open**.

- Locate your chosen photo and click **Open**.

  The photo opens in the workspace.

Using a preset Filter Gallery effect

PhotoPlus comes complete with preset effects which can be applied to a layer to quickly transform it. Let's apply a watercolour effect now.

To add a Filter Gallery effect:

1. On the **Layers** tab, right-click the **Background** layer and select **Duplicate**.

2. In the **Duplicate Layer** dialog, rename the layer 'Paint' and click **OK**.

   The new layer is added to the Layers tab.

3. On the **Layers** tab, right-click the new **Paint** layer and select **Convert to Filter Layer**.

4. On the Photo Studio toolbar, click  **Filter Gallery**.

The **Filter Gallery** dialog will launch displaying a preview of your photo and the **Artistic** category open by default.

5. From the **Artistic** category, click **Watercolour II**.

The effect is applied to your preview and its controls display in the **Filters** tab.

▽ ▣ Watercolour II ↶ ☒
Accuracy: ▬▬▬▬▬▬▽▬▬▬▬ 70

We want to keep as much detail in the painting as possible, so we need to adjust the filter's settings.

6. On the **Filters** tab, drag the **Accuracy** slider to 100.

The preview of the effect updates.

7. Click **OK** to apply the effect to your photo.

The effect has lost too much detail, so to bring back some of the original photo we'll reduce the Paint layer's opacity.

8.   On the **Layers** tab, ensure the **Paint** layer is selected and the reduce the **Opacity** to **60%**.

This resulting watercolour effect might be just what you're looking for. If so, you can export your watercolour and begin sharing it (see *Saving & Exporting* on p. 187 for more information). However, we're going to define some of the painting's detail and make the watercolour more authentic.

Save now! Click **File > Save As** and choose a new name for your file.

When saving, you may receive a warning message recommending you save your file as a PhotoPlus picture. Click **OK** to save as an .spp file so you can modify changes at a later date if necessary.

See *Filter Gallery* on p. 207 for other inspirational effects you can apply using the Filter Gallery.

Define lines

We'll apply another filter effect to another duplicate layer to redefine some of the photo's original lines and bring back some detail.

To add an effect from the Effects menu:

1. On the **Layers** tab, right-click the **Background** layer and select **Duplicate**.

2. In the **Duplicate Layer** dialog, rename the layer 'Lines' and click **OK**.

    The new layer is added to the Layers tab.

3. On the **Layers** tab, right-click the new **Lines** layer and select **Convert to Filter Layer**.

4. From the **Effects** menu, select **Edge>Find All**.

    The filter effect is immediately applied and you can see the lines through the Paint layer.

5. On the **Layers** tab:

- Drag the **Lines** layer so it sits above the **Paint** layer.

- Set the **Lines** layer's blend mode to **Multiply**.

- Reduce the **Opacity** to **35%**.

  The watercolour now includes sketch lines as well as paint.

Next we'll add a texture to the watercolour to give the illusion it is painted on canvas.

 Don't forget to save your work!

Creating a patterned surface

To create the illusion that the watercolour appears on canvas, we'll add a new layer to our project with a pattern on it.

To add a patterned layer:

1. On the **Layers** tab, click ⊞ **New Layer**, and in the **Layer Properties** dialog, rename the layer 'Pattern' and click **OK**.

    The new layer is added to the Layers tab.

2. From the **Edit** menu, select **Fill**.

3. From the **Fill** dialog:

    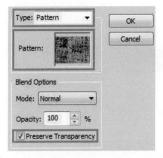

    *   From the **Type** drop-down list, select **Pattern**.

    *   Click the **Pattern** swatch and then from the drop-down list, select the **Bumps – Weaves** category.

- From the displayed swatches gallery, select the second swatch from the first row.

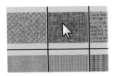

- Ensure the **Preserve Transparency** option is selected.

- Click **OK** twice to exit the dialogs and return to the main workspace.

4. On the **Layers** tab, select the **Pattern** layer and change the blend mode to **Soft Light**.

A wonderful canvas texture is applied to the painting.

However, due to the pattern's colour, the painting has acquired an undesirable tint.

 Don't forget to save your work!

To desaturate a layer:

1. With the **Pattern** layer still selected, on the **Adjustments** tab, click Hue/Saturation/Lightness.

2. Reduce the **Saturation** level to -100.

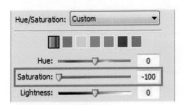

The adjustment has now removed all the colour from all underlying layers.

We want to apply the adjustment to only affect the layer below (i.e. the Pattern layer) rather than all the layers—we'll do this by clipping the adjustment to the layer below.

To clip to layer:

- On the **Layers** tab, right-click the **Hue/Saturation/Lightness** layer, and select **Clip to Layer Below**.

The clipping is indicated by indentation and the 🔃 icon.

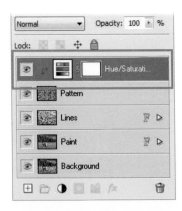

The adjustment now only affects the layer below, restoring the photo's original colours.

To put the final touches to the watercolour, and make it more authentic, we'll add a border.

 Don't forget to save your work!

Adding a custom border

In order for the border to work correctly, we will need to use a group and a mask. Although this might seem daunting at first, we'll take you through the steps and show you just how simple it can be.

In a real watercolour, the white background may come through where the painter has not painted right up to the edge of the canvas. The first phase of creating this effect is to add a plain, white background. To place this underneath the current Background layer (i.e. the original photo), we need to promote the Background layer.

To promote to layer:

• On the **Layers** tab, right-click the **Background** layer, select **Promote to Layer** and, in the **Layer Properties** dialog, rename the layer 'Original'.

Now we'll add a new background layer.

To add a new background layer:

1. On the **Layers** tab, click the  New Fill or Adjustment Layer and select **Fill Layer**.

2. In the **Layer Properties** dialog, rename the layer 'Canvas' and click OK.

3. In the **Edit Fill** dialog, click the colour swatch.

4. In the **Colour Selector** dialog, in the H, S and L input boxes, type '0', '0', and '100', respectively (i.e. HSL=0, 0, 100).

5. Click **OK** twice to return to the workspace.

6. Drag the **Canvas** layer so it sits underneath the **Original** layer.

   The Layers tab should now look this:

Now we'll expose the Canvas layer at the edges. However, we only want to affect some of the layers—e.g. we still want the Pattern layer fully visible to give the Canvas layer some texture too. We can do this by grouping the middle layers.

To create a layer group:

- On the **Layers** tab:

  - Click the **Lines** layer.

  - Hold down the **Ctrl** key and then click the **Paint** and **Original** layers.

    All three layers should now be selected.

  - Right-click the selected layers and click **Group Layers**.

With the group now in place, we can add a mask which will expose the Canvas layer.

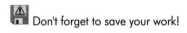 Don't forget to save your work!

To add and edit a group mask:

1. On the **Layers** tab, select **Group 1** and then click ⬜ **Add Layer Mask**.

2. On the Tools toolbar, select 🖌 **Paintbrush Tool**.

3. On the **Colour** tab, set the foreground colour to black.

4. On the **Brush Tip** tab, from the category drop-down list, select **Media - Paint**, and then select the **Grainy** brush tip.

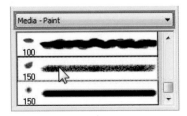

5. Paint a rough border around the painting.

6. Continue to paint the border, varying the size, type and opacity of brush used, until you are happy with the results.

We used a combination of **Round07 (Basic)**, **Splodgy (Media - Paint)**, and **Blot07 (Effects - Grunged)**.

 If you make a mistake along the way, on the **Colour** tab, switch the foreground colour to white and repaint over the mistake.

There you have it! A photo transformed into a beautiful, authentic looking watercolour.

 Don't forget to save your work!

 Exporting your completed image to a common image file format will allow you to get full use from it. See *Saving & Exporting* on p. 187 for more information.

 See *Brushes* on p. 199 for other inspirational ways to use PhotoPlus's brush tips.

Final Touches

With your adjusted photos or creative projects now complete, you're almost ready to show them to family, friends, clients and the rest of the world. Before you do so, there are a few final touches you may wish to add to your photos to fully prepare them for printing or electronic distribution.

Stylized Edges

 20 min

You've spent a long time taking your photos and tweaking them in PhotoPlus to get them looking fantastic, but before you share them, you may wish to add some stylized edges to them.

By the end of this tutorial you will be able to:

- Quickly access preset edges and frames from the Macros tab.

- Create rounded edges using a vector mask.

- Create a feathered edge using a layer mask.

Let's begin...

1. On the Standard toolbar, click 🗁 **Open**.

2. Locate your chosen photo and click **Open**.

    The photo opens in the workspace.

Frame and edge macros

PhotoPlus includes a range of professionally designed frames and edges you can add to your photos with the click of a button. These presets are located in the Macros tab and might be just what you're looking for. We'll quickly look at these before creating our own custom edges.

To apply a macro:

*   On the **Macros** tab:

    *   From the drop-down list, select the **Frames**, **Layout Blurs**, or **Vignettes** category.

    *   Select a macro from the list.

    *   Click the ▷ **Play** button.

The macro runs and your photo is updated with the selected frame or edge.

Next we'll look at applying our own custom rounded and feathered edges...

 Save now! Click **File > Save As** and choose a new name for your file.

 When saving, you may receive a warning message recommending you save your file as a PhotoPlus picture. Click **OK** to save as an .spp file so you can modify changes at a later date if necessary.

Rounded edges

Rounded edges are a great way of styling your finished photo. To maintain flexibility in our approach to creating this edge effect, we'll first convert the Background layer to a standard layer.

To promote a layer:

1. On the **Layers** tab, right-click the **Background** layer and click **Promote to Layer**.

2. In the dialog, click **OK** to accept the default settings. The layer is renamed **Layer 1**.

We'll now use a vector mask to create your round edged photo.

To add a vector mask:

1. On the Tools toolbar, from the QuickShape Tools flyout, select ▢ **Rectangle**.

2. On the context toolbar, click ⊟ **Paths**.

3. Click and drag the rectangle shape so it fills the entire photo area.

4. Click and drag the shape's node downwards to modify the width and type of corner (the node is located on the left).

5. From the **Layers** menu, select **Vector Mask>Create from Path**.

A vector mask is added to the Layers tab.

Your photo instantly adopts rounded edges with a transparent background showing through.

You can modify the rounded edges at any time by editing the vector mask...

 Save now! Click **File** > **Save As** and choose a new name for your file.

To modify a vector mask:

1. On the **Layers** tab, ensure the vector mask is selected (it should display a white border)—if it is not selected, click the mask's thumbnail.

2. On the Tools toolbar, from the Node Tools flyout, select the ▷ **Node Edit Tool** and click on the photo to select the rectangle.

3. Click and drag the shape's node up or down to modify the width and type of corner (we increased the rounded edge).

 For more information on vector masks, search *Using vector masks* in PhotoPlus Help.

 Don't forget to save your work!

If you export your photo as it currently is (see *Saving & Exporting* on p. 187), it will produce an image with either a white or transparent background, depending on your settings.

Alternatively, you can add a black (or white) or coloured background to emphasise the rounded corners.

To add a new fill layer:

1.   On the **Layers** tab, click the **New Fill or Adjustment Layer** and select **Fill Layer**, and, in the **Layer Properties** dialog, click OK to accept the default settings.

2.   In the **Edit Fill** dialog, click the colour swatch.

3.   In the **Colour Selector** dialog, select a colour using the Hue slider and the Saturation and Lightness colour box.

4.   Click **OK** twice to return to the workspace.

     A new fill layer is added to the Layers tab.

5.   On the **Layers** tab, drag **Layer 2** down so it is positioned underneath **Layer 1**.

     The coloured corners now display through the transparent areas exposed by the crop.

Now you know the technique of creating rounded corners, let's move onto feathered edges.

Don't forget to save your work!

Feathered edges

Feathered (or blurred) edges give a soft border around your photos. The feathering can fade to transparency or any chosen colour. To maintain flexibility in our approach to creating this edge effect, we'll first convert the Background layer to a standard layer.

To promote a layer:

1. On the **Layers** tab, right-click the **Background** layer and click **Promote to Layer**.

2. In the dialog, click **OK** to accept the default settings. The layer is renamed **Layer 1**.

Now our photo is located on a standard layer we can mask it to create our feathered edges. First, we need to create a selection to work from.

To create a selection:

1. From the Tools toolbar, from the Shape Selection Tools flyout, select the ⬚ Rectangle Selection Tool.

2. Click and drag the rectangle selection so it fills most of the photo area but leaves a gap with the photo edge.

We'll now feather the selection and then create a mask to achieve your feather edged photo.

To feather selection then mask:

1. On the context toolbar, click **Modify Selection**.

2. In the **Modify Selection** dialog:

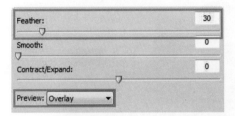

- From the **Preview** drop-down list, select **Overlay**.

  This will help you visualise the feathering effect.

- Increase the **Feather** slider (we set ours to **30**).

- Click **OK**.

3. On the **Layers** tab, click  **Add Layer Mask**.

A mask is added to the layer.

Your photo updates so everything within the selection is displayed, everything outside the selection is hidden and there is a feathered transition between the two.

If you export your photo as it currently is (see *Saving & Exporting* on p. 187), it will produce an image with either a white or transparent background, depending on your settings.

Save now! Click **File** > **Save As** and choose a new name for your file.

As with rounded edges, you can add a black (or white) or coloured background to emphasise the feathered effect. See *To add a new fill layer* on p. 173 for more information.

Copyrights & Captions

20 min

Placing a visual copyright or caption on your photo is a great way of identifying your work and protecting it from unauthorized use. We'll walk you through several ways of placing a copyright or caption onto your photo, using text and brushes.

By the end of this tutorial you will be able to:

- Add a caption using a shape layer and text layer.

- Use a custom brush to quickly add copyright information to a photo.

Let's begin...

- On the Standard toolbar, click  Open.

- Locate your chosen photo and click **Open**.

  The photo opens in the workspace.

Creating a caption

Placing a caption onto a photo is as simple as placing text on top of the photo, but if you combine it with one of the QuickShape Tools you can avoid any clashes between text and photo.

To add a QuickShape:

1. On the Tools toolbar, from the QuickShape Tools flyout, select
   ▢ Rectangle.

2. On the context toolbar, click ⊟ Shape layer.

3. On the **Colour** tab, click ▪ **Reset Colours** to set the foreground swatch to black.

4. Click and drag across the bottom of the photo.

A rectangle QuickShape is added to the photo as a new shape layer.

5. On the Tools toolbar, select the **T** **Text Tool**, and then click and drag to define the size of the text object, ensuring it will fit comfortably over the previously created shape.

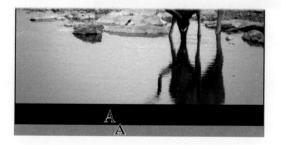

6. Type your text and then, with the **Text Tool** still selected, click and drag to highlight the text.

7. On the context toolbar:

    •   Select a font from the drop-down list.

    •   Adjust the size of the text as necessary.

    •   Click the colour swatch and, in the **Colour Selector** dialog, select a colour using the Hue slider and the Saturation and Lightness colour box, then click **OK**.

        The text object will update to your chosen settings.

8. On the Tools toolbar, select the ⊹ **Move Tool** and then position the text within the boundaries of the shape.

This might be exactly what you need, but we'll tweak the shape layer's opacity to add a touch of style!

💾 Save now! Click **File > Save As** and choose a new name for your file.

To adjust layer opacity:

- On the **Layers** tab, select the shape layer and reduce the **Opacity** to **50%**.

The results add a simple but very professional caption to your photo.

To speed up the process of adding identical text to your photos (such as a copyright), you can create a brush from any text and paint it onto your photos. We'll look at this next.

 Don't forget to save your work!

Creating a copyright brush

You can use PhotoPlus to create a brush which you can then use to paint a copyright onto your photos. Let's create one now, starting with a new document.

To create a new document:

1. From the **File** menu, click **New**.

2. In the **New Image** dialog:

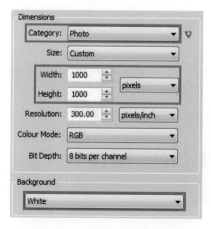

*   Set the **Category** to **Photo**.

- Set the **Size** to **1000 x 1000 pixels**.

- Set the **Background** to **White**.

- Click **OK**.

  A new blank document opens.

We'll create a brush which includes the copyright symbol and some text, but you can use virtually anything you want to, to create your brush.

To add text to the image:

1. On the Tools toolbar, click the **T** **Text Tool**.

2. Click on the image to add an insertion point and then:

   - Hold the **Alt** key and type '0169' using the numpad, release the **Alt** key.

     A copyright symbol will be placed on the image.

   - Type your name or company name.

3. (Optional) Click and drag to highlight your text and then, on the context toolbar, change the font and size of the text to fill the width of the image.

   We chose **Georgia**, **36 pt**.

©Anna Sassin

Your text is now ready for conversion to a brush.

Save now! Click **File** > **Save As** and choose a new name for your file.

To convert text to a brush:

1. On the Tools toolbar, from the Shape Selection Tools flyout, select the
   Rectangle Selection Tool.

2. Click and drag a rectangular selection around your text.

3. On the **Brush Tip** tab, right-click in the gallery and selection **Add Category**.

4. In the **Category** dialog, type 'Watermark' and click **OK**.

   A new, blank category is added to the Brush Tip tab.

5. Right-click in the blank gallery and select **Define Brush**.

6. In the **New Brush** dialog, type 'Copyright' and click **OK**.

   Your selection is converted to a brush using default settings.

7. On the **Brush Tip** tab, right-click the newly created **Copyright** brush and select **Brush Options**.

8. In the **Brush Options** dialog, from the **Attributes** section, select **Spacing** and then increase the **Spacing** to 500.

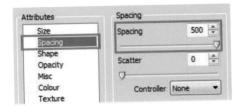

This will ensure that, when you use the brush, you will only add one set of the text with every click.

9. Click **OK** to exit the dialog and update the brush settings.

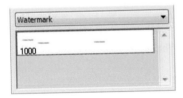

Search *Creating your own brush tips* in PhotoPlus Help for more information.

Now we have our brush, let's use it to add a copyright to our photo!

To 'paint on' a copyright:

1. On the Standard toolbar, click 📂 **Open**.

2. Locate your chosen photo and click **Open**.

   The photo opens in the workspace.

3. On the **Layers** tab, click ⊞ **New Layer**, and then, in the **Layer Properties** dialog, click **OK**.

🔖 To speed up the process, you can skip the above step and paint directly onto your photo. This would be a destructive approach, so ensure you work on a copy of your photo and save or export to a new name. See *Saving & Exporting* on p. 187.

4. On the Tools toolbar, select the 🖉 **Paintbrush Tool**.

5. On the **Brush Tip** tab, select **Watermark** from the category drop-down list, and then select your **Copyright** brush.

6. On the context toolbar, reduce the **Size** of the brush as needed to fit comfortably on your photo (as below).

7. Click once on an unobtrusive part your photo to paint your copyright.

The copyright is clear but does not detract from the photo. It can be quickly added to all your photos—simply repeat the process of opening them and painting.

 Save now! Click **File** > **Save As** and choose a new name for your file.

> Exporting your completed image to a common image file format will allow you to get full use from it. See *Saving & Exporting* on p. 187 for more information.

Saving & Exporting

🕐 5-15 min 🖊🖊🖊🖊🖊

If you've spent a long time correcting your photos in PhotoPlus, or you've created some fantastic graphic art, you'll want to be able to save it and share it with others! This tutorial shows you exactly how to achieve this.

By the end of this tutorial you will be able to:

• Save your work as a PhotoPlus project file.

• Create a high quality JPEG (JPG).

• Export a copy of your work to various image formats.

• Resample your work on export to meet various output size requirements.

Let's begin...

Depending on the type of project you've been working on, there are several options open to you when you come to save, either saving as a PhotoPlus project file, overwriting your original photo*, or exporting to a new image. We'll look at these in detail now.

 Hopefully, before you start working on your files, you'll have copied the original photos to somewhere safe. This way you'll always have a set of "digital negatives" or untouched files that you can return to.

 *We really don't recommend overwriting the original file unless you are 100% confident that you will not want to make changes in the future.

Saving as a PhotoPlus project file

 When you save your work as a PhotoPlus project file, you save the entire project and its settings, such as adjustment layers, masks and paths. If you want to keep the layers editable to make changes later, save your image as a PhotoPlus project (***.spp**). You can open, edit and resave a PhotoPlus project file as many times as you want without any loss of quality.

To save your work as a new PhotoPlus project:

1. From the **File** menu, click **Save As**.

2. If you only have a single, **Background** layer and no paths or masks, select PhotoPlus Pictures (*.spp) from the **Save as type** drop-down list, type a name for your file and then click **Save**.

    - or -

If you've already added any layers, paths or masks, you will see a new dialog asking you to save as a PhotoPlus picture. Click **OK** and then type a name for your file and click **Save**.

Creating a high quality JPEG (JPG)

When you've completely finished editing your photo (be it JPEG or a raw photo processed by the Import Raw dialog), one of the best ways to save your changes is to create an entirely new copy of the photo, i.e. "export" it. This way, you can leave your original file intact. A popular format to export to is a high quality JPEG.

 For more information regarding raw and JPEG files, search *Introduction to raw images* in PhotoPlus Help.

To export an image to a high quality JPEG:

1. From the **File** menu, select **Export**.

2. In the **Export Optimizer** dialog:

• Set the **Format** to JPEG File (JPG).

- Set the **Quality** to **95%** (recommended*).

- Click **Export**.

 *When you are working with a photo that has not been edited before, reducing the quality of a JPEG to 95% can result in a file size that is half the size of a JPEG exported at 100%! The loss in image quality due to compression is undetectable to the human eye.

3. In the **Save As** dialog, type a name for your file and click **Save**.

Your JPEG image is saved to the location you specified and ready to print and share!

 If you've been working on an existing photo (raw or JPEG), any Exif information stored within the original photo is automatically added to the exported file.

File size and image quality

It is possible to reduce the file size of photos (for electronic transfer or placing on websites) by changing the JPEG quality settings. One thing to remember is that as JPEG compression is lossy, i.e., it "throws away data", the photo quickly begins to degrade, especially at lower settings.

You can preview the effect that changing the quality settings (and selecting different file formats) has on your photo and the exported file size in the Export Optimizer dialog. We'll use the photo of the bird to see this in action.

To preview photo export quality:

1. From the **File** menu, select **Export**.

    The **Export Optimizer** dialog opens, displaying your photo along with the estimated exported file size at the selected quality settings.

2. Click ⊕ **Zoom In** to zoom into your photo.

3. Experiment with different types of output file (from the **Format** drop-down list) and **Quality** settings to see the effect that they have on your photo's appearance and file size.

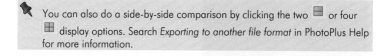

You can also do a side-by-side comparison by clicking the two ▱ or four ▦ display options. Search *Exporting to another file format* in PhotoPlus Help for more information.

If you look at the images below, you can see the effect that changing the export quality has on the photo. All examples are zoomed in to 400%. The original 12 megapixel photo JPEG (4288 x 2848) had a file size of 4.15MB.

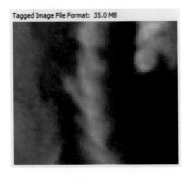

Tagged Image File Format (TIF)

This is the quality experienced using one of the industry standard TIF file types. TIF uses lossless compression and is very good if you still intend on doing some work on the file and don't want to save it as a PhotoPlus project.

It is sometimes used as an intermediate step for raw images before exporting the final image as a high quality JPEG.

As you can see, the file size is 35MB!

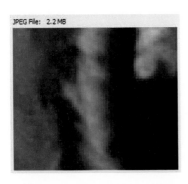

JPEG File (JPG) at 95% quality

This is the quality experienced with a JPEG export set to 95%. As you can see, by comparing it to the image above, it looks virtually identical (remember, this is at a zoom level of 400%!).

Look at the file size... only 2.2MB! Interestingly, at 100% quality, the file size created is 5.1MB, more than double!

(Sometimes a good compromise is a setting of 98%).

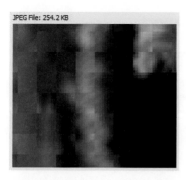

JPEG File (JPG) at 10% quality

This is the quality experienced with a JPEG export set to 10%. The degradation in image quality is pretty horrendous.

The file size has been reduced to 254KB (0.25MB) but the image looks very poor. If you need to display small images on the web, you would be better resampling them and actually reducing the dimensions of the image (and as a result, the file size also decreases).

For more information on resampling, see *Resizing & Resampling* on p. 15.

 For graphics or drawings (but not photos), try the **Portable Network Graphics (PNG)** format. It produces very small files for images which have crisp lines and relatively few continuous tones. Unlike JPEG, it also supports an alpha (transparent) channel. The format is also lossless, meaning that there is no degradation in quality, no matter how many times you edit and re-save the file.

Resampling a photo on export

Most photos taken straight from the camera have dimensions much
bigger than the average monitor display. This means that we can reduce
the file size by resizing the photo to fit the screen. Also, as the resolution
doesn't need to be as high for a screen image, it means that we can
further reduce file size by exporting the image as a lower quality JPEG,
without affecting the appearance too much. We can do all of this in one
step with the **Export Optimizer**. Let's do that now.

The photo we are using is a 12 megapixel image taken from the 2011
Isle of Man TT. The image measures 3359 x 2333 pix and has a file size
of 3.9MB. We are going to resample it ready for uploading to our
website.

It is also beneficial to upload a smaller version of your photo to your web
page if you are worried about someone "stealing" it. If you resize the photo to
800x600, while it will look okay on screen, it won't be any good for printing.

If you are creating images as desktop wallpaper, why not resample them to
the specific desktop resolution they are intended for?

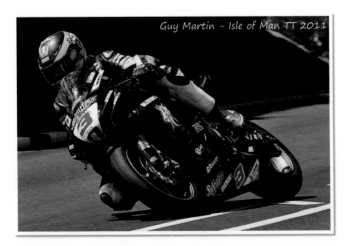
Guy Martin - Isle of Man TT 2011

To resize a photo with the Export Optimizer:

1. From the **File** menu, click **Export**.

    The dialog displays your photo along with the estimated exported file size at the selected quality settings.

    We'll set the size of the image first.

2. In the **Size** section:

    *   From the **Method** drop-down list, select **Lanczos 3 Window**.

    *   Set the **Width** to **800** Pixels and press the **Tab** key. (The **Height** updates automatically.)

        Notice that the estimated file size has decreased dramatically. In our example, the file size has gone from 5.1MB (5100KB) down to around 0.38MB (380KB)!

3. (Optional) If we reduced the JPEG quality setting to 95%, that file size drops to 220KB (0.22MB), yet there's hardly any difference in visual quality!

4. To complete the export, click **Export**, type a name for your file and click **Save**.

   Your photo is saved to the chosen folder and is ready to be uploaded to your website or sent via email. (The original remains unchanged.)

 If you want to increase the dimensions of your photo, you may want to do this using the **Image Size** dialog from the **Image** menu. This way you'll be able to apply any necessary sharpening before you export the file. For more information on resampling, see *Resizing & Resampling* on p. 15.

 Thumbnails

Thumbnails are smaller versions of the same picture. They are very small, in both file size and viewing size, and are often used on websites to link to the larger, high quality version of the image. The small file size means that even a page containing many thumbnails will load very quickly in a browser. The example below is a 150 x 99 pixel thumbnail created from our original image using the Export Optimizer. The file size is only 10.4K!

Creative Showcase

PhotoPlus X6 provides many preset brushes, corrective adjustments, and filter effects you can apply to your photos to create stunning compositions and pieces of art. Sample files are also included to inspire you!

Brushes

PhotoPlus provides a large collection of creative brush tips for you to get creative with and use with your photos. These brushes are stored in **Basic**, **Calligraphic**, **Effects**, **Media** and **Stamps** categories in the **Brush Tips** tab.

To select a brush tip:

1. On the Tools toolbar, select 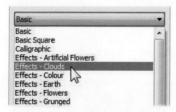 **Paintbrush Tool**.

2. On the **Brush Tip** tab, from the category drop-down list, select a category.

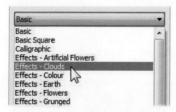

The category's gallery is displayed in the tab.

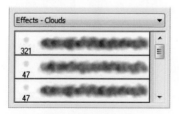

Each gallery shows the brush tip and stroke. The number indicates the brush tip's default diameter.

3. Click to select a preset brush tip from the gallery and then click and drag across your photo to paint your lines.

We'll showcase the **Effects - Clouds** (as selected above), **Media - Paint** and **Media - Spray** sub-categories next.

Effects - Clouds

Media - Paint

Media - Spray

Samples

PhotoPlus is installed with sample files which show how the program can be used to modify photos or create stunning digital art. These sample files are available directly from the **Startup Wizard**.

To open a PhotoPlus sample file:

- From the **Startup Wizard**, in the **Open** section, click any file named with the suffix - **Sample**.

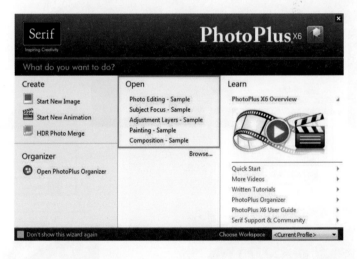

 The Startup Wizard's **Open** section displays recently used files only. The sample files will eventually disappear from the list. Therefore, in a standard install, the files can also be accessed from the following location:

C:\Program Files\Serif\PhotoPlus\X6\Samples, or
C:\Program Files (x86)\Serif\PhotoPlus\X6\Samples

We'll showcase the **Photo Editing, Painting** and **Composition** samples next.

Photo Editing

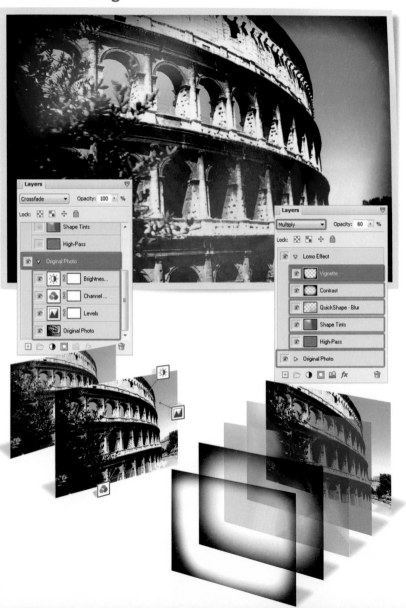

Painting

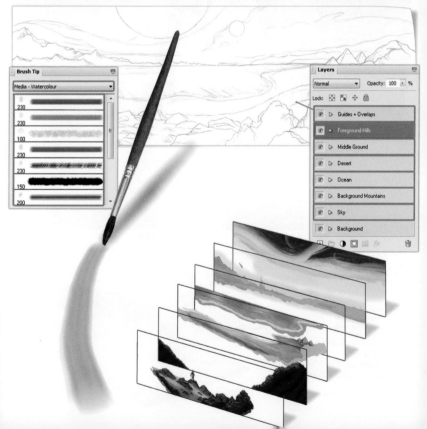

Composition

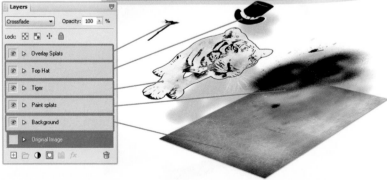

Filter Gallery

The Filter Gallery offers an environment for applying single or multiple filter effects. The expandable categories (including **Distort, Blur, Sharpen, Edge, Noise, Render, Stylistic,** and **Artistic**) have a thumbnail gallery displaying the range of effects available.

To add a Filter Gallery effect:

1. On the Photo Studio toolbar, click **Filter Gallery**.

    The **Filter Gallery** dialog will launch displaying a preview of your photo and the **Artistic** category open by default.

2. Click ⊞ to open a category on the right, and click a gallery thumbnail to apply the effect to your photo.

For more information about the Filter Gallery, search *Using the Filter Gallery* in PhotoPlus Help.

Stylistic: Stained Glass

Artistic: Pencil

Artistic: Watercolour II

PhotoFix

PhotoFix provides an environment that simplifies the often complicated process of photo correction. A range of ready-made presets are included in the **Favourites** tab.

To add a PhotoFix preset to your photo:

1. On the Photo Studio toolbar, click **PhotoFix**.

    PhotoFix will launch displaying a preview of your photo.

2. From the **Favourites** tab, click to apply one of the **Lighting** or **Creative** presets.

> For more information about PhotoFix, search *Using PhotoFix* in PhotoPlus Help.

Lighting

Original Image

Intense

Warmer

Sapphire

Sepia

Black and White

Creative

Metropolis

Glamour

Old Photo

Intense Sepia

Etching